What a God we Christians have!

Glenn W Baxter

Scripture Truth Publications

WHAT A GOD WE CHRISTIANS HAVE!

This book is based on material previously broadcast in the "Truth for Today" progamme on London's Premier Radio between August 2005 and January 2010.

First published 2011
Typeset and transferred to Digital Printing 2011
ISBN: 978-0-901860-59-0 (paperback)
Copyright © 2011 Scripture Truth Publications

Cover photograph ©iStockphoto.com/garyforsyth

Published by Scripture Truth Publications
31-33 Glover Street,
Crewe, Cheshire, CW1 3LD
Scripture Truth is an imprint of Central Bible Hammond Trust, a charitable trust
Typesetting by John Rice
Printed and bound by Lightning Source

FOREWORD

I first met Glenn Baxter in the late 1960s when we served together as officers at a boys' camp near Holy Island in Northumberland. It was clear from our first meeting that he was committed to excellence in everything, putting all he had into even the apparently most insignificant aspects of his life – treating each task as service for the Lord Jesus Christ. The look of devastation when my team beat his to win the team trophy remains with me to this day – but he never held it against me!

We met up again many years later in Lancashire, where his tireless efforts in Christian work with both young and old in Southport and beyond were greatly appreciated.

In more recent years, we shared a common purpose in driving forward the literature work of *Scripture Truth Publications* (STP), and all the trustees benefited from the balance of consideration and enthusiasm he brought to his work as chairman.

His major concern was to build up the faith of young Christians, and his addresses were always intensely practical and challenging. For some years Glenn had been one of the regular broadcasters on the *Truth for Today* radio programme. When the trustees of STP looked back on Glenn's ministry we felt that it would be fitting to collect his radio ministry and make it available to all. We wondered how many radio talks he had delivered. Perhaps as many as ten? Imagine our delight when we discovered that he had given seventeen radio talks in all.

So here they are. Listening to Glenn was never a comfortable experience: there was always a very direct challenge in what he said, that in itself confirmed the value of his ministry. Glenn was a great lover of the Authorised (King James) Version of the Bible, and it is used throughout this book. And the title? Read *Elijah – the Champion of God* or Peter Ollerhead's closing words in the *About the Author* section and all will become plain!

I have applied as light a touch as possible in preparing the transcripts of Glenn's radio talks for publication, to retain the immediacy of the spoken word. They could have been grouped by topic or Testament, but presenting them simply in the order in which they were broadcast reveals interesting links which are worth maintaining.

I do hope your enjoyment in reading this book is as great as mine in preparing it. Read it with care. Think about what you read. Don't try to take in too much at a time. But then – **Do what it says!** For, without doubt, what Glenn would have looked for as his greatest legacy was not a book, but a generation of Christians sharing his excitement at "what a God we Christians have!"

John Rice
July 2011

CONTENTS

WHAT A GOD WE CHRISTIANS HAVE!

Christ as seen in the offerings

SERIES: CHRIST IN ALL THE SCRIPTURES (LUKE 24:27)

BROADCAST DATE: 7TH AUGUST 2005

If we were giving an overall summary of the Bible, we might simply say that:

- *the Old Testament* outlines events before Jesus was born;

- *the Gospels* tell of Christ's coming into this world and His life, death and resurrection;

- then *the Epistles* contain teachings for Christ's followers;

- and, finally, *the book of Revelation* shows Christ revealed throughout time with particular details about Christ in relation to future events.

Does this mean that there is nothing of Christ in Scripture before the Gospels? Not a bit of it! The Old Testament is full of Christ, fulfilling Luke 24:27 when Jesus, while walking with two people towards the village of Emmaus, began at Moses and all the prophets and expounded unto them in **all** the Scriptures the things concerning Himself.

To look at the topic of Christ as seen in the *tabernacle*, we would deal with Scriptures mainly in the book of Exodus. Here we will look at Christ as seen in the *offerings*, considering mostly Scriptures in the next Bible book, Leviticus.

The order of the books in the Bible is important. Exodus tells us of God's people being redeemed and having a new relationship with Him. Leviticus moves from that basis to show how the redeemed people can approach God in worship and have fellowship with Him by living lives appropriate to their new relationship with God and that worship. So, in verse 1 of Leviticus, God speaks to His people from the tabernacle, right in their midst, and not, as in Exodus, from the top of a mountain.

The first 7 chapters of Leviticus are taken up with our subject of the offerings. The 5 offerings are outlined up to chapter 6:7 and then further details to help the offerer are set out from 6:8 to the end of chapter 7; these further details are usually referred to as *the law of the offerings*.

The 5 offerings are:

- the *burnt* offering;
- the *meal* offering;
- the *peace* offering;
- the *sin* offering;
- the *trespass* offering.

The first three are often called the *sweet savour offerings* and the last two the non-sweet savour offerings, dealing as they do with sin and trespass. All the offerings were primarily for God, in the way and in the sequence which He instructed. The idea was that the aroma of the offering would rise up to God and be acceptable to Him.

Now let's look at each of these offerings, remembering that our emphasis is on seeing Christ in these Old Testament offerings.

THE BURNT OFFERING

First, the *burnt* offering in Leviticus 1 and 6:8-13. Let's note some of the key aspects in chapter 1 regarding this first offering:

verse 3	it had to be a male without blemish;
verse 5	it had to be killed before God;
verse 5	there is great emphasis on the blood;
verse 6	it had to be flayed, that is, its skin had to be removed;
verses 7 & 8	the prominence of fire;
verse 9	every part of the animal had to be clean.

All of these key aspects relate to the burnt offering of a bullock. From verse 10 to the end of the chapter, you can see that a sheep or goat or dove or pigeon could be chosen to be offered instead. Many of those key aspects are repeated for these other animals. So what do these key aspects tell us?

As often is the case, we need to go to the New Testament to get our answers. The longstanding couplet about the Old and New Testaments is absolutely true:

> *The Old is by the New revealed;*
> *The New is in the Old concealed.*

In Hebrews 9:14, the writer pens the words,

"the blood of Christ, who through the eternal Spirit offered himself without spot to God."

9

In Ephesians 5:2, Paul writes,

> "Christ also has loved us and has given himself for us an offering and a sacrifice to God for a sweet smelling savour."

Jesus prayed to God the Father (Luke 22:42),

> "Nevertheless not my will, but thine, be done."

The New Testament epistles have phrases referring to Jesus such as "in him is no sin" (1 John 3:5), "Who did no sin" (1 Peter 2:22); "who knew no sin" (2 Corinthians 5:21).

Christ clearly is pointed forward to in the burnt offering. Christ was perfect, without blemish, both inwardly and outwardly. He was slain and His blood was shed firstly to and before God. He suffered and bore the consequences of God's holy wrath against sin, answering the flaying and the fire of Leviticus 1.

It is important to note that the burnt offering is the very first of these offerings. Christ came first and foremost to accomplish God's will and to glorify God through what He achieved in His death. In the burnt offering, the whole animal was offered; Christ was wholly for the will and pleasure of God. This is of such importance and delight to God, and He places this sacrifice first.

Remember that the animals which could be offered for a burnt offering varied in size from a bullock, a large animal, to a much smaller dove or pigeon. Whether a believer's appreciation of the worth of Christ is large or small, God wants us to bring that appreciation to Him in worship, because God delights in every heart-felt expression of the perfections of Christ.

THE MEAL OFFERING

Now the second of the offerings, the *meal* offering, is found in Leviticus 2 and 6:14-23. This is sometimes called the *meat* offering as in the Authorised Version of the Bible; the NIV refers to it as the *grain* offering.

In Leviticus 2:1, this meal offering is to be composed of fine flour, oil and frankincense – to which verse 13 says that salt should be added. Verse 11 specifically states that leaven, or yeast, must *not* be used. There is great emphasis in the chapter on fire and burning and on baking in the oven or frying pan.

Where is Christ in all this? In Romans 12:1, Paul urged Christians to

"present your bodies a living sacrifice, holy, acceptable unto God."

Christ's perfect life, devoted to God, is our supreme example for this. I would like to suggest that it is to this perfect, devoted life of Christ that the meal offering points forward.

The meal offering had to be of fine flour, that is with no lumps or foreign parts. Christ's life was always perfectly consistent. Christ had no strong points – *everything* He did or said was perfect and equally strong. In Scripture, oil is often a picture of the Holy Spirit. So in the oil of verses 1 & 4, we see that Christ was conceived of the Holy Spirit and anointed by the Holy Spirit. The sweetness and fragrance referred to in the frankincense of verses 1 & 2 were seen in Christ's lovely life. Salt in verse 13 keeps things wholesome – and how wholesome was Christ's life. Leaven is always used in Scripture to speak of things that are evil. There was to be no leaven in the meal offering and there was no sin in Christ's life.

11

The wonderful perfections of Christ's life are often seen in times of *pressure* and that is what the fire, the oven and the frying pan would remind us of.

Can I mention, in passing, that blood was not involved in the meal offering. The meal offering was a sweet savour to God (see verses 2 & 9) and, while Christ's life was pleasurable to God, His perfect life did not bring about redemption. It needed His blood shed at Calvary to achieve that.

THE PEACE OFFERING

We come now to the third offering, the *peace* offering in Leviticus 3 and 7:11-34, the last of the 3 sweet savour offerings. The NIV calls this the *fellowship* offering.

In the original language, peace means not only being in agreement, but also in prosperity, unity and happiness. This offering was a banquet of fellowship with some part of the offering for everyone. God's part, the fat, came first – from 3:3 onward. The fat is the inward, the richest part. We benefit hugely from the sacrifice of Jesus on the cross but, in fact, the first benefit is for God – only God can appreciate fully the inward worth of Jesus and of what He did. God desires fellowship with man, but only on the basis of what Jesus did.

Note also how often the blood is mentioned in this chapter. There is no peace with God without the blood of a sacrifice.

After God had His part, there was a part for the priests: the breast and right thigh (7:31-32). The breast speaks of the love of Jesus and it was to be waved before God. We can show to God that we appreciate the love of Christ. The thigh is important in walking and reminds us that Jesus lived here in love and we take that as our example. Being heavier than the breast, the thigh was heaved up and down by the priest before God, again to demonstrate to God an appreciation of it. These are sometimes called *wave* offerings and *heave* offerings.

Lastly, the offerer takes the remainder of the sacrifice and shares it with others who appreciate the value of the offering.

Ephesians 2:14 says that

"he (Christ Jesus) is our peace."

Colossians 1:20 says,

"Having made peace through the blood of his cross."

Both these Scriptures in Ephesians 2 and Colossians 1 go on to say that Jesus, by His death on the cross, has brought about our reconciliation to God and so we have access to the Father (Ephesians 2:18) and have fellowship with the Father, with the Son and with fellow believers (1 John 1:3). All of this is through Christ and what He has done – how wonderful that we have a picture of all that in Leviticus 3.

THE SIN OFFERING

The fourth sacrifice is the *sin* offering and the Scriptures are Leviticus 4 and 6:24-30. The first three sacrifices speak particularly of the inward perfections of Christ but here He takes on the sin of others and so this is the first of the two non-sweet savour offerings.

The Bible makes it clear that God can't have anything to do with sin. It is abhorrent to His holy nature.

"God is light, and in him is no darkness at all" (1 John 1:5).

13

So the bullock in Leviticus 4:12 had to be burnt outside the camp, well away from the Holy Place which represented God's presence. Any sin is an act against God's holy nature and so the sin offering covered sins of ignorance – see verse 2.

What a solemn and amazing thing it is to read in 2 Corinthians 5:21 that

"he (God) hath made him (Jesus) to be sin for us, who knew no sin."

Jesus was the only person ever to have lived on this earth who never sinned in anything that He did or said or thought. When He died for our sin, He had to go into the distance away from the holy God and so He called from the cross,

"My God, my God, why hast thou forsaken me?"

But how necessary it was, because it was only through the perfect sacrifice of Jesus that a holy God could forgive sinners and still be righteous. It is to Christ that Leviticus 4 pointed forward. Little wonder that twice in our verses in chapter 6 it says of this offering that "it is most holy."

It is interesting to note the order of the offerings for sin in chapter 4: first for the priest a bullock, then for a ruler a male goat kid, then for an ordinary person a female goat kid or lamb. Taking on responsibilities for God demands an increased sense of sin and the value of Christ's offering for it. The priests needed to offer a sacrifice for their own sin, unlike Christ who died for the sin of others. The priests had to keep on offering these sacrifices for sin, whereas Jesus died for sin once. Hebrews 10:12 says:

"This man … offered one sacrifice for sins."

THE TRESPASS OFFERING

The fifth offering is the *trespass* offering in Leviticus 5, 6:1–7 and 7:1-7. This is the second of the non-sweet savour offerings.

There are both similarities and differences between the sin and trespass offerings. Perhaps the differences can best be summarised by looking on the sin offering as dealing with *my nature*, the root cause of the problem, whereas the trespass offering deals with *what flows out from my nature* in wrong deeds, words or thoughts. These offences are first of all against God and infringe His rights as seen in chapter 5, but then they can go on to cause problems and injury to other people, as is clearly described in the first few verses of chapter 6. Trespass is a form of sin and any sin causes hurt. In order to make restoration to God and to those people who had been wronged, the one trespassing had to add 20% to the offering and to the restitution – see 5:16 and 6:5.

In seeing Christ in this trespass offering shall we just let Scripture speak for itself?

- Romans 4:25: "(Christ) was delivered for our *offences*" (the same word in the original as 'trespasses').
- 2 Corinthians 5:19: "God was *in Christ*, reconciling the world unto himself, not imputing their trespasses unto them."
- And on the matter of *restoration*, Psalm 69:4: "then I restored that which I took not away."

Just in passing, you will see that the order of the offerings differs slightly in the first 5 chapters of Leviticus compared with the law of the offerings in chapters 6 and 7, where the peace offering comes last. This is because

15

the law of the offerings is looking at things from man's side, not God's side, and, with man, sin and trespass have to be cleared before there is any thought of peace.

TWO OTHER OFFERINGS

We ought to note that there are two other offerings in the Old Testament.

The Drink Offering

One is the *drink* offering which occurs most frequently in Numbers, particularly 15:1-13, but also in other Old Testament books. This was a mix of oil and wine and was not drunk but poured out at the time the burnt offering or meal offering was made. In the Bible, wine speaks of joy and so the drink offering would tell us of our joy, and indeed God's joy, as we contemplate the value of the obedient death and the wonder of the perfect life of Jesus.

The Red Heifer

The other offering is that of the *red heifer*. This is recorded in Numbers 19 at the time when the Children of Israel had left Mount Sinai and had resumed their journey through the wilderness towards the Promised Land. The book of Numbers is all about the walk and service of God's people, redemption having been pictured in the events recorded earlier in the first half of Exodus. In their journeyings, God's people failed frequently, so damaging their relationship with God. The purpose of the offering of the red heifer was to restore that relationship.

In a Christian's walk, failure occurs and there is defilement from the world around. These things don't put at risk our eternal salvation but they can damage the joy of our relationship with God our Father. Thus the value of

1 John 1:9 comes in:

> "if we confess our sins, he is faithful and just to forgive us our sins, and to cleanse us from all unrighteousness."

That forgiveness and cleansing is based on the eternal value of the work of Christ at Calvary.

THE MESSAGE OF THE OFFERINGS FOR TODAY

The Old Testament offerings contained God's instructions as to how His *earthly* people should approach Him and worship Him at that time. Christians are God's *heavenly* people and our worship now is a spiritual and not a physical matter, as it was then. They didn't then have the Holy Spirit permanently living in them. The Holy Spirit does dwell permanently in born again Christians today and God's desire is that we now offer our worship to Him as Father in Spirit and in truth (John 4:23-24). The Bible teaches that every Christian is a priest and has access to God to make that sacrifice of praise. Just as in the offerings in Leviticus there was a portion identified as being for the priest, so, even though this is not the prime objective, the Christian always gains from offering to God.

So, there are many general lessons that we can learn from these Old Testament offerings and truly all Scripture is profitable (2 Timothy 3:16). But I believe that the over-riding lesson is that in our spiritual offerings to God, **Christ comes first**. Christ and His work are the basis of God's pleasure and our blessing. In our worship of God, He wants to see us make much of Christ.

1 Corinthians 16

SERIES: THE CHURCH, THE BODY OF CHRIST AND ITS HOPE

BROADCAST DATE: 19TH MARCH 2006

We will look at the final chapter, number 16, of the first letter to the Corinthians. After considering this chapter, we will conclude by summarising very briefly the teaching of the whole letter.

The great and fundamental teachings of chapter 15 concern the resurrection of Christ and its consequent hope for the church. It may seem an anti-climax that, immediately after this, the apostle Paul deals in chapter 16 with matters which, in comparison with the tremendous truth of the resurrection, seem relatively trivial. But it is dangerous for us to look on any part of the Word of God as trivial since we are told that all Scripture is given by inspiration of God and is profitable (2 Timothy 3:16). We remind ourselves that 1 Corinthians is one of the main sources of teaching in the Bible as to how the local church should conduct itself and it is the Holy Spirit of God who brings these matters in chapter 16 to the attention of the church, then and now.

To help structure my comments, I would like to group the verses in chapter 16 into five sections:

verses 1-4	church collections;
verses 5-12	Paul's, Timothy's and Apollos' plans;
verses 13-14	exhortations;
verses 15-18	serving the saints;
verses 19-24	the closing greetings.

CHURCH COLLECTIONS (VERSES 1-4)

One of the reasons for Paul writing this letter was to respond to a series of questions raised with him by the Corinthians – see 7:1. Here at the start of chapter 16 Paul turns to another of these questions, this time relating to church collections. Paul emphasises that giving should be a normal part of the life of any church, not just for special occasions. From verse 2 we see that the giving should be:

- *regular* ("upon the first day of the week");
- *individual* ("every one of you");
- *systematic* ("lay ... in store");
- *proportionate* ("as God hath prospered him").

So, giving is expected of every believer, whatever their financial resources may be. And that giving requires thought and should not be haphazard. If I get an increase in pocket money or grant or salary or pension, I take that as God prospering me and I should readily want to return part of that to Him. What part that may be is between the Lord and me. In the Old Testament times, the part was legally fixed at one tenth – a *tithe*. In this time of grace, there is no fixed part specified by Paul or anyone else in Scripture. Rather, my response should be in the context of the greatness of the free grace shown to me by God.

It is interesting that the church collections were on the first day of the week – Sunday – the Lord's Day. This was a crucial day in the early church's weekly calendar. Acts 20:7 tells us that they met on the Lord's Day to break bread in remembrance of the Lord and His death. The Lord's Day reminds us of Christ's resurrection – a time of new beginnings. It is a day of response from God's people to Him and appropriate that this should include the response of giving financially to the Lord's work.

It would seem from these first four verses that the believers in Corinth were collecting for the poor saints in Jerusalem; a fitting response from one group of believers to another – all part of the one body of Christ. The responsibilities for collecting and delivering the gift were all local, though Paul would help if they wished. As already instructed in 14:40, all things were to be done in an orderly fashion and so in verse 3 Paul instructs that more than one representative from the church in Corinth should be responsible for delivering the gift to Jerusalem.

Paul's, Timothy's and Apollos' plans (verses 5-12)

All three of these men devoted themselves full time to the Lord's service and it is important to note the factors that governed the plans which they made. It is clear from these verses that all of them looked to the Lord for His guidance. In a sense their plans were flexible as they sought to see precisely what the Lord had in mind for them and exactly when and where. When presented by the Lord with an opportunity, Paul made maximum use of it – see verse 9. We see another good example of this in Acts 16:6-12, where Paul journeyed west, not certain quite where God wanted him to go as the Holy Spirit closed door after door, until he received a message to go to Macedonia. He went immediately. Little wonder that blessing followed both in 1 Corinthians 16:9 and in Acts 16:14-15 & 33-34. Where God works, the devil is never far away in opposition, as indicated by verse 9 of our chapter and Acts 16:16-24.

Paul was an apostle and Apollos wasn't, but Paul did not impose his will on Apollos, as verse 12 indicates. Each servant of the Lord is answerable only to the Lord. We aren't told why Apollos did not wish to go to Corinth at that time, but he may have been sensitive to not wishing to stir up any further divisive feelings in Corinth of the sort referred to in chapters 1 and 3 where some in the Corinthian church were saying "I follow Apollos". How needful for a servant of God to be sensitive! And how good to see that Paul and Timothy and Apollos showed neither rivalry nor criticism of each other. A servant should never seek to magnify himself or his own position.

EXHORTATIONS (VERSES 13-14)

The third section contains five exhortations, which are as appropriate today as when written.

1.   *Watch* – be constantly alert to detect any attack by the enemy against God's truth as set out in the Bible. That attack may be either direct or subtle, the latter requiring particular vigilance. In this letter, Paul points out a host of ways in which the enemy had been successful in bringing into the church all sorts of evils which the Corinthians had not detected because they were not in a watchful frame of mind.

2.   *Stand fast* in that truth – be stable to preserve it whatever the cost.

3.   Act like men – *be courageous* – don't be cowards.

4.   *Be strong* through the inward strength supplied by God. Ephesians 3:16 speaks of the need to be strengthened with might by the Spirit in the inner man.

5.   *Do everything*, yes literally everything, *in love.*

I understand that all of these exhortations imply not one-off actions but continuous actions. So I need to watch and keep on watching, stand fast and keep on standing fast, and so on.

SERVING THE SAINTS (VERSES 15-18)

Just a reminder that in the New Testament the *saints* are God's people. The instant a person becomes a born-again Christian, God calls him or her a saint, someone who is *set apart* for His holy purpose.

As far as I can tell, Stephanas is mentioned only in 1 Corinthians. From verse 15 of our chapter we see that he and his family were the first converts in Achaia, which is the southern part of what we now call Greece and in which Corinth was situated. From 1:16 we see that Paul had baptised Stephanas and his household, and from 16:15 we are told that the household of Stephanas had addicted or devoted themselves to serving the saints. The local church at Corinth had not appointed them to undertake that service; they themselves before the Lord had determined that this would be their area of service for Him. We are not told precisely what that service involved but it would be wide ranging and demanding – in verse 16 it is described as *labouring*.

Also in verse 16, Paul endorses the value of serving the saints and encourages the believers in Corinth to take account of the qualities of Stephanas and those like him.

Paul goes on in verses 17-18 to underline how he himself had been refreshed and rested by a visit from Stephanas and Fortunatus and Achaicus. Not everyone at Corinth accepted Paul's teaching, even though he was an apostle. He must have been dismayed by that. But here were three brothers in the Lord from Corinth who *did* value God's word and who set out to encourage Paul, thereby serving one of God's people.

What an encouragement and challenge the verses in this section are. We can't all be great teachers or preachers but surely in various ways we can all serve the saints, encouraging them and benefiting the whole of the local fellowship with whom we meet. Seeing my fellow-believers as saints of God somehow elevates their standing and makes it a privilege to serve them.

THE CLOSING GREETINGS (VERSES 19-24)

In Bible times Asia broadly was what we now call Turkey. Paul was writing from Ephesus which was in the then Asia and he conveys the greetings of the surrounding churches to the believers in Corinth.

He also passes on the warm greetings of Aquila and his wife Priscilla who, of course, would know many of the Christians at Corinth as they had lived there – see the beginning of Acts 18. It is outside the scope of this talk, but I do recommend to you a study of this lovely Christian couple. They are referred to six times in the New Testament, always together, always attached to the Lord's people wherever they lived, always serving the Lord – a fine example to all Christian couples.

Despite the problems at Corinth, all the Christians in the region were prepared to add their greetings to those of Paul. It's a good thing to keep loving our fellow-Christians even when difficulties arise between us!

In verse 20 Paul encourages them to greet each other with a holy kiss. I understand that it was, and still is, normal in that part of the world for people, whatever their sex, to greet each other with a kiss. It would be the equivalent of the handshake in this part of the world. Just note out of interest how careful the Holy Spirit is to guard against any excesses: the kiss of greeting must be *holy*.

Paul must normally have dictated his letters but we see from verse 21 that he personally writes these last few words, perhaps to avoid any doubts as to whether the letter actually comes from him.

Verse 22 is very solemn. Only those who have a real love for the Lord Jesus Christ – His full title – belong to Him. All others shall be cursed – see the word *anathema* in the Authorised Version of the Bible, which should be followed by a full stop. In the Authorised Version the next word is *maranatha* which means the Lord will come, not maybe but certainly. A great certainty for the believer but a solemn warning of future judgement for those who at the time of their death, or at the coming of the Lord, do not know Him as Saviour.

I appeal to any reader who has not yet taken Jesus as Saviour and Lord to do so while there is time. The Bible does not teach that there is an opportunity to avoid judgement once death has occurred or the Lord has come.

Verse 23 is Paul's normal ending to his letters to the churches in the New Testament. How lovely to see that in this case he adds verse 24. Despite the fact that many at Corinth had rejected him and his teaching, he wants the final words to be that he still loves them in Christ Jesus. Paul's enduring love for all the people of God is crystal clear throughout his writings.

REVIEW OF THE TEACHING OF 1 CORINTHIANS

The letter was written by Paul to the whole church at Corinth. In the very first verse of the letter Paul underlines the fact that he is an apostle and therefore what he says carries authority. While he is writing to respond to specific questions raised with him by the Corinthians, Paul judges it essential first of all to deal, in the first six chapters, with matters more fundamental to the spiritual state of the church at Corinth than those questions which they raised. Those fundamental matters included an emphasis on spiritual as opposed to human wisdom, the need to be united in Christ and not be divided in following different human figures, the fact that only God reveals things of heaven, an underlining of the only foundation on which Christian service and reward can be based and the need to identify and deal with any form of immorality in the church.

Even when, from chapter 7, Paul does turn to deal with the Corinthians' specific questions, he extends his comments to encompass wider spiritual aspects which have a bearing upon the questions being raised. Isn't it amazing that this church which had so many problems and deficiencies should receive such marvellous writings as the meaning of the Lord's Supper in chapter 11, the wonder of love, as perfectly seen in Christ, in chapter 13 and the extensive consideration of the fact and consequences of Christ's resurrection in the longest chapter in the book, chapter 15.

Everything points to the church at Corinth being large in numbers, with many intellectuals in the company. By the standards of the world they would be a successful church – big in numbers and high in intellect. But in terms of true spirituality they were desperately low. See 3:1-3 for the apostle Paul's summary of their spiritual state. There he describes them as infants, immature in spiritual things, not capable of digesting the meat of the truth of God, still following the principles of the men of the world.

Can I give you my personal impressions of three of the main messages of 1 Corinthians? First, I am struck by *the authority which Paul attaches to the teaching of the book*. As I said previously, right at the start of the letter he states his apostleship but he re-emphasises that from time to time, for example in chapters 4 and 9. This authoritative writing is addressed to the whole church at Corinth and is a pattern as to how the church there should operate. But not only the church in Corinth – also, as in the words of 1:2,

> "all that in every place call upon the name of Jesus Christ our Lord."

Nowhere does it suggest that the teaching of 1 Corinthians should alter over the centuries as political, social and moral attitudes change. The church today should be as subject to the teaching of all of 1 Corinthians as the church at Corinth ought to have been in AD 60 or thereabouts. The challenge for each Christian today is whether the fellowship of believers with whom he or she meets does indeed accept and follow all of this authoritative teaching.

My second over-all impression from 1 Corinthians is *how easy it would be to arrive at a false impression of the spiritual state of any Christian fellowship*. It would be so easy to look at outward appearances such as existed with the church at Corinth – a large number of people attending, a high level of intellect, an ability to conduct eloquent debates. I hasten to say that I am not suggesting for one moment that there is an inherent problem with large numbers or with good intellect or with eloquence. But 1 Corinthians brings home to us the fact that these things which naturally appeal are not necessarily the marks of true spirituality. Paul emphasises that the Corinthians were actually very weak spiritually, despite outward appearances. They needed to view things from God's, not man's side, to have heavenly, not earthly, wisdom, to understand and obey God's unchanging pattern for the conduct of church matters and to live in love with each other. I ask myself, what is the true spiritual health of the local Christian fellowship of which I am a part?

The third and last of these personal impressions is *the marvellous way in which Paul wrote to these believers at Corinth, balancing on the one hand a forthright stand for the truth of God and correcting the Corinthian believers, with a true love for them on the other hand.* He starts by thanking God for them in 1:4-8, throughout his letter he calls them "brethren" and, as we have seen, his very last words to them in 16:24 emphasise his love for them in Christ.

Some of us perhaps are inclined to let things pass on the grounds of love. Others of us may veer in the opposite direction and seek to stand for truth but in a completely unloving manner. May we be challenged to display the balance of truth and love which Paul showed in this letter. In John 1:17 it says that

"grace and truth came by Jesus Christ."

In Jesus there was a perfect balance between showing grace and displaying truth.

I trust that God will have blessed our consideration of 1 Corinthians and that the Christian church, wherever represented, may seek to follow the instructions set out in this book, part of the Word of God which lives and abides for ever (1 Peter 1:23).

Matthew 13:1-43

SERIES: CLUSTERS OF PARABLES

BROADCAST DATE: 25TH JUNE 2006

A *parable* has been described as *an earthly story with a heavenly meaning.* It must have been terrific actually to hear the Lord Jesus tell those stories. We thank God that we have the record of them in the Bible. Each individual parable told by Jesus is a gem in its own right. Like a precious stone, the more a parable is considered, the more delight it gives. When precious stones are placed in a cluster each stone retains its own value but there is also an inter-play between each stone in the cluster so that the over-all impression is enhanced. In a similar way, I trust that we will see that there are added heavenly meanings when God puts a number of parables together in His precious Word.

There is a cluster of seven parables in Matthew 13. In the Bible, the number 7 generally speaks of completeness or perfection and so in Matthew 13 the seven parables give a complete view of the kingdom of heaven. Sometimes in the Bible a group of seven items can be divided into four and three or three and four: for example, the letters to the seven churches in Revelation chapters 2 and 3. So it is in Matthew 13 where there is a clear break after the fourth parable. Jesus tells the first four parables to anybody who will listen. But in verse 36, He sends the multitude away and the last three parables are then spoken only to the disciples. Those first four parables, then, deal with *the external world aspect* of the kingdom of heaven and the last three parables with *the divine mind* on the kingdom of heaven.

We can therefore divide consideration of Matthew 13 and its seven parables into the first four parables and the last three. Our subject here is the first four.

Verse 11 of our chapter tells us that the subject of the chapter is *the kingdom of heaven*. So what is the kingdom of heaven? The structure and content of our chapter give us some clues. We will see as we touch on each of the first four parables that the kingdom of heaven is a wide concept, not limited to true believers only, not just the Church, but is the whole sphere of Christian profession, encompassing the real born again believers in Jesus as well as those who are not real but professors only.

The end of Matthew 12 is a real watershed. Up to that point, Jesus has spoken in a straightforward way to everyone. In 12:47-50 Jesus indicates that His family is not the Jews or any with whom He had earthly ties, but His spiritual family is made up of all those of whatever nation or background who have a spiritual link with His Father (12:50).

When we come to chapter 13, therefore, for the first time in Matthew, Jesus speaks many things in parables – see 13:3. Up to now the Lord had used what could be called parables only rarely, for example once in chapter

7 and twice in chapter 9. When, as recorded in Matthew 13:10, the disciples ask why this extensive use of parables now, Jesus explains in verses 11-16 that the mysteries contained in the parables are for the ears and hearts only of those in His new family, those with the spiritual capacity to understand these things. Those outside that family have no spiritual perception at all. This message is reinforced by the fact that Jesus goes on to explain the meanings of the first two parables, but those explanations are given only later to the disciples and not to the general multitude.

THE PARABLE OF THE SOWER (VERSES 3-9)

The first parable recorded in Matthew 13 is also recorded in Mark 4 and Luke 8. The words of the parable are contained in verses 3-9:

> "Behold, a sower went forth to sow; and when he sowed, some seeds fell by the way side, and the fowls came and devoured them up: some fell upon stony places, where they had not much earth: and forthwith they sprung up, because they had no deepness of earth: and when the sun was up, they were scorched; and because they had no root, they withered away. And some fell among thorns; and the thorns sprung up, and choked them: but the other fell into good ground, and brought forth fruit, some an hundredfold, some sixtyfold, and some thirtyfold. Who hath ears to hear, let him hear."

So, the parable tells of a sower going out to sow seed. At that time, of course, a farmer would spread the seed by hand with the inevitable result that the seed would land on a variety of grounds. Jesus mentions four grounds in His story: the *way side* or the *path side* in verse 4, the

WHAT A GOD WE CHRISTIANS HAVE!

stony ground in verse 5, the *thorny ground* in verse 7 and the *good ground* in verse 8.

The nature of the ground on which the seed landed determined what happened to the seed. The seed that fell on the path side landed on hard ground and would not be able readily to penetrate the soil, so giving an easy meal to the birds. No crop there for the farmer! The seed that fell on stony ground in verse 5 landed on a place where the soil was shallow. The seed germinated and had early promising signs but as soon as the full blast of the sun brought difficult conditions, the poor roots caused by the shallow soil could not support the plant and it withered and died. Again, no crop for the farmer! Thirdly, some of the seed fell on thorny ground. The thorns grew and choked out the plants. Once again, no crop for the farmer! But in verse 8 some of the seed fell on good, fertile ground and produced a good or even excellent crop.

Jesus explains the parable of the sower (verses 18-23)

Jesus went on to explain to His disciples the meaning of this first parable. As with many instances in the Gospels, we have to take together all the three mentions of this parable in the Gospels to obtain a full explanation, because each writer was guided by the Holy Spirit to record only what was necessary for that writer's inspired presentation of a particular aspect of the Lord Jesus and His work. Luke 8:11 states that "The seed is the word of God". Jesus explains in Matthew 13:19 that the way side or the path side ground is a picture of someone not understanding the Word and the wicked one, Satan, snatches away what is sown, just like the birds snatched away the seed. In verses 20-21, Jesus explains that the stony ground with its shallow soil is a picture of some-one who initially receives the Word with joy and it looks at first as though the Word has taken root, but as soon as trouble or opposition arises, that person falls away. Third comes the explanation in verse 22 about the thorny ground. Here the seed or the Word is choked out by the cares of normal life and the pleasure and glamour of riches. But lastly in verse 23, there is the good ground which is like the person who genuinely receives and understands the Word and goes on to bear fruit for God. The reality of taking in the seed is tested by the fruit it bears.

Now, this first parable is the basis for the six which follow. As already mentioned, the end of Matthew 12 is a watershed in this Gospel. Jesus moves from addressing His old family, the Jewish nation, to spreading the Word, like a farmer sowing, to anyone who hears, to use the words at the beginning of verse 19. At the very start of the chapter, Jesus moves out of the limited confines of a house to address openly the wide multitude by the sea side. Seas in the Bible tend to speak of all the nations of the world and all this emphasises the widening of the spreading of God's Word from this point. Those who are going to understand "the mysteries of the kingdom of heaven" (see verse 11) are limited to those who really do receive the Word of God, that is, the seed falling on the good ground, the true believers existing amongst the wider multitudes.

Having established that basis, Jesus goes on to tell another three parables to the multitudes and then a further three to the disciples only.

THE PARABLE OF THE WHEAT AND TARES (VERSES 24-30)

The second parable in Matthew 13 describes a man who sowed good seed in his field. While people slept, the man's enemy sowed tares or weeds among the good seed. When both lots of seed developed into plants, the servants asked the man from where the weeds had come and the man told them that the source of the problem was an enemy. The servants asked whether they should pull up the weeds but the man said not to do this in case, in the process of pulling up the weeds, the wheat might be damaged. Instead, he instructed his men to leave the two sorts of plant growing together until harvest time when the weeds would be separated and bound together and burned, while the wheat would be gathered into his barn and kept.

Jesus explains the parable of the wheat and tares (verses 36-43)

Jesus then explains to His disciples the meaning of this second parable, which is recorded only in Matthew. What a clear explanation it is, leaving no room at all for ambiguity. Jesus said that the man sowing is Himself, the Son of Man, a title Jesus frequently uses of Himself throughout the four Gospels. The field is the whole world; good seeds are the true children of the kingdom; the weeds are the children of the wicked one; the enemy who sowed the weeds is the devil; the harvest is the end of the world; the reapers are the angels. Jesus states that at the end of the world He will send His angels to gather out of His kingdom all offenders and doers of iniquity and they will be cast into a furnace of fire, no doubt the lake of fire mentioned in Revelation 20:15. It would be a time of desperate, hopeless sorrow for them. But on the other hand, verse 43 is a tremendous verse for believers in Jesus because at that time they, made righteous by the blood of Jesus and faith in Him, will "shine forth as the sun in the kingdom of their Father".

Please note in verses 38 & 41 further evidence that the kingdom of heaven is a wide concept incorporating both true believers and those who are not true. In verse

38 it says that the field is the whole world, not just the church. In verse 41 those who are not true are gathered out of that kingdom.

So, this second parable in the cluster builds on the first. The idea of the sowing of seed is continued but now there are two sowers. Jesus, the Son of Man, continues to sow the good seed but the other sower now introduced is the devil who sows the weeds. The results of these sowings continue mixed together until the time of harvest when the two shall be separated, each going to a totally different destination.

THE PARABLE OF THE MUSTARD SEED (VERSES 31-32)

In this third parable in the chapter, Jesus likens the kingdom of heaven to a grain of mustard seed sown by a man in his field. Mustard seed is tiny but from that tiny beginning the plant grows until it becomes a large tree in which birds come and find shelter.

Around the edges of my garden there are three or four fairly large trees in which a number of birds rest or even build their nests. Some of those birds are very welcome but many, such as magpies and pigeons, certainly are not, causing problems to smaller birds and to my vegetable patch! In this third parable, Jesus was illustrating how the kingdom of heaven would grow and provide a resting place for all sorts of individuals, some of whom would cause problems. Remember in the first parable of the chapter that the seeds that fell by the way side were eaten by birds thereby stopping any crop from those seeds. In verse 19 Jesus says that those birds are like the wicked one, Satan, who snatches away the true seed, the Word of God, before it can develop in the heart. Similarly in this third parable of the mustard seed, Satan will use individuals who are not true believers in the

Lord Jesus but who come within the growing kingdom of heaven and are used by Satan to cause problems.

THE PARABLE OF THE LEAVEN (VERSE 33)

In the fourth parable, the kingdom of heaven is said by Jesus to be like leaven, or yeast, mixed by a woman in a large amount of meal or flour until the leaven permeated the whole mixture.

I have a clear picture in my mind how, many years ago, my mother would make bread from time to time. The whole house was filled with the lovely aroma of baking bread. I remember going with my mother to the local chemist's shop where she bought a small amount of yeast which she then mixed thoroughly with quite a lot of flour. You couldn't then see the yeast but the effect of it was certainly there as the baking bread expanded in size.

In the Bible, whenever leaven is mentioned, it always speaks of *evil*. For example, in Leviticus 2:11,
"No meal offering, which ye shall bring unto the LORD, shall be made with leaven";
in 1 Corinthians 5:6 and Galatians 5:9,
"A little leaven leaveneth the whole lump";
in 1 Corinthians 5:7,
"Purge out therefore the old leaven, that ye may be a new lump, as ye are unleavened".

When it says in Matthew 13:33, that the kingdom of heaven is like leaven it means that the kingdom of heaven is like the whole of this fourth parable, not the element of leaven. Within the kingdom of heaven there is the corrupting presence of evil, not always clearly visible, but its effect is there. We can see it, for example, when we look around the world at the wide group of people who call themselves Christians but some of whom blatantly disobey God's Word in its teaching and/or its practice.

THE OUTWARD ASPECTS OF THE KINGDOM OF HEAVEN

So, to sum up. These first four parables are spoken by Jesus in front of the multitude. In the Bible, the number 4 often speaks of the world – mankind with its weakness. We often use the phrase, "the four corners of the earth" and there are four earthly dimensions: north, south, east and west. These first four parables of the cluster of seven give us therefore the *outward aspects* of the kingdom of heaven:

1. In the parable of the sower, the seed, the Word of God, is spread before everyone who will hear.

2. The parable of the wheat and the tares or weeds, shows that at the same time as the Divine Sower sows the Word of God, the enemy, Satan, is sowing false seed and the fruit of the two seeds will be harvested at the end, each fruit having a different destination.

3. The parable of the mustard seed shows how the kingdom of heaven grows to an abnormal size because of the activities of the wicked one and houses those who cause problems.

4. In the parable of the leaven the evil character of the leaven is shown – introduced to the flour by the woman but affecting the whole mixture.

We see, therefore, that there is a progression as the Lord reveals further details about the kingdom of heaven as He relates each parable in the cluster.

Can we notice the presence of Satan and evil in each of these first four parables? Satan's work (2 Corinthians 4:4) is to

> "blind the minds of them which believe not, lest the light of the glorious gospel of Christ, who is the image of God, should shine unto them".

Putting it bluntly, dear reader, Scripture is telling us that if you are not a Christian, Satan is doing his best to keep you in that position. That is his objective. Like the birds in the parable of the sower, when the seed of the Word of God is spread, he tries to snatch it away before it can find a resting place in your heart. Jesus calls Satan the father of lies (John 8:44) and Satan will use any sort of lie to stop you accepting Christ as Saviour. It is for individuals to respond to God's Word which is why Jesus says in verse 9 of our chapter: "Who hath ears to hear, let him hear."

But Satan doesn't stop there. As our cluster of parables teaches us, Satan actively sows false teaching. He causes those who are not real believers to shelter within the professing church and to spread that false teaching and the evil attaching to it. There is a solemn warning here to true Christians to be on their guard constantly against this activity of the enemy. We need to know our Bibles and base our beliefs and practices only on what God sets out in His Word. That is a challenge to all of us and we need to be aware of it. You will see from the second parable that the enemy caused the damage "while men slept" (Matthew 13:25). May we be preserved from allowing falseness and evil to creep in to our churches because we are not alert!

I trust that the Lord will help us appreciate the wonder of His divine stories, each one amazing, and having added wonder when put together in a cluster.

Hold fast the form of sound words - 2 Timothy 1:13

SERIES: PASSING ON THE TORCH

BROADCAST DATE: 15TH OCTOBER 2006

It was at the 1936 Olympic Games in Berlin that the modern Olympic torch relay was first instituted. More than 3,000 runners carried the Olympic flame from Olympia to Berlin, each runner being responsible for carrying the torch for a particular distance and then passing it on to the next. What a tragedy for a runner if the torch went out while it was within his responsibility! Each runner would be keen to ensure that the flame kept burning and was safely passed on to the next.

Each believer in every generation of Christians has had passed down to him or her the precious truth of God. It is each Christian's responsibility then to hold on to that truth, to witness to that truth and to pass it on to the next generation.

We are going to base what we have to say on Paul's writings to Timothy. Paul was not Timothy's natural father but he did refer to Timothy as his spiritual son – see 1 Timothy 1:2 & 18 and 2 Timothy 1:2. Paul had a great

Christian love for Timothy and valued his support. He held up Timothy as an example to other Christians, for example in 1 Corinthians 16 and in Philippians 2. Under God's guidance, Paul sent Timothy to Ephesus to deal with matters of concern in the church there. It seems that Timothy was inclined to be rather timid and may not have been too strong physically. Paul wanted him to understand the truth, to teach it and to stand firmly for it. In effect, Paul, the older Christian man, was passing on the torch of truth to the younger man, Timothy, and was encouraging him in turn to pass it on to others at Ephesus.

Paul's second epistle to Timothy is most relevant to our subject. You may have noticed in your reading of the Bible that Paul's second letter to a church or to an individual usually demonstrates a decline in spiritual circumstances from the time of the first letter. Paul's first letter to Timothy had given teaching on sound doctrine, on godliness and on how those comprising a church ought to conduct themselves, and Timothy was instructed to pass on that teaching to the church at Ephesus. Of course the teaching was also set out as instruction for us today. In Paul's second letter to Timothy, the emphasis is on how Timothy and every other individual believer should walk in a time when adherence to the truth of God had declined. The second letter is particularly touching because it is generally accepted that it is the last letter written by Paul and so we have his final recorded words to his son in the faith, Timothy.

So, as we turn to our subject, we consider it in the context of the challenge to each Christian to be willing to accept the torch of truth passed down to him or her, to hold it firmly in a time of general turning away from the truth of God as set out in His Word, and to pass it on to others to hold in the future until the Lord returns for His church. Paul wrote to Timothy (2 Timothy 2:2):

> "The things that thou hast heard of me …, the same commit thou to faithful men, who shall be able to teach others also."

While our particular subject is the first seven words in 2 Timothy 1:13, "Hold fast the form of sound words", I would like us to read and consider the whole of the verse:

> "Hold fast the form of sound words, which thou hast heard of me, in faith and love which is in Christ Jesus."

I would like to divide this verse into four phrases and to think separately of each.

THE FORM OF SOUND WORDS

First of all, let us think about the phrase "the form of sound words". Another way of expressing this could be "the pattern of wholesome words". Now, there are some important messages in this phrase. When Paul referred to the form or pattern he meant that Timothy should have clearly in his mind an outline of the truth of Scripture, knowing that truth and not allowing himself to deviate from it. What is more, the phrase tells us that this outline of truth is based on *actual words passed down* to Timothy and to us. What and where are these words? Surely not just some vague reference to traditions passed down, the accuracy and reliability of which may be open to challenge. No, the words are right in front of us, the very words of Scripture which we can study knowing that the words are not just Paul's or Peter's or James' words but are words divinely inspired

41

by the Holy Spirit – see 2 Timothy 3:16. These are the words from which you and I are instructed to form the outline of truth to hold.

And Paul tells us that these words are sound or whole-some words – literally, *healthful* words. 1 Timothy 4:6 tells us that a good servant of Jesus Christ is "nourished up in the words of faith and of good doctrine." We all know the importance of nourishing food in giving healthy physical bodies. The words of Scripture gener-ate healthy Christian lives. Dear reader, never be frightened to quote *actual words of Scripture*. Obviously at times we have to try to explain what those words mean but don't let us water down the words even with the laudable objective of making them easier to under-stand. The truths behind some Bible words or phrases – for example, "glory", "grace", "the only begotten Son" – are just not capable of definition because the meaning is so deep. By all means let us try to explain them, but let the words and phrases themselves stand, to be increas-ingly, but never in this life fully, understood by believers as they meditate on them!

WHICH YOU HAVE HEARD OF ME

The phrase "the form of sound words" is followed by "which thou hast heard of me". In taking on and passing on the torch, what message do I take from this next phrase? I think that Paul is emphasising his authority as an apostle and is guarding against the danger, in these times of spiritual decline, that we take our teaching from any source other than the Word of God. Paul and every other apostle wrote with divinely-inspired author-ity and we must take their written words as being from God Himself. Please note that it is the *words themselves* which are inspired, not just the general thoughts.

There are no apostles of this sort now. Paul was in a unique position in that he was called by the Lord from heaven as recorded in Acts 9. It was a requirement of all of the apostles that they should have seen the Lord – see Acts 1:21-22 and 1 Corinthians 9:1. The Bible does not teach that there are successors to those apostles. Evidently, even in the early days of the church, there were those who falsely claimed that they were apostles – see Revelation 2:2. The book of Revelation closes with a most solemn warning to anyone who adds to or takes away from the words written in Scripture. Please note again that the warning in Revelation 22:18-19 refers to the actual written words of Scripture, the same idea as in our verse in 2 Timothy. The Holy Spirit wants to guard the very detail in the inspired words left on record for us and, in passing on the torch, He wants us to know and guard the actual words of Scripture.

There is a verse in the short epistle of Jude which is of great relevance to our subject. It is Jude 3, part of which reads:

> "it was needful for me to write unto you, and exhort you that ye should earnestly contend for the faith which was once delivered unto the saints."

The force of those last few words is that we should fight to defend the body of truth which was *once for all* passed on to believers. This reinforces what we have just been saying. The truth which we have in Scripture was delivered by the apostles as a complete statement never to be added to. Jude goes on in verse 4 to say why he needed to make this exhortation. There were certain men who had crept in to the churches and were spreading teachings which were not in accord with the truth of God. These were ungodly men who had perverted

God's grace into lawlessness and immorality and were denying the Lord Jesus Christ. Some Christians refer to this as a time of apostasy – a falling away from a professed position once taken. Jude urged believers to contend or fight to maintain allegiance to the body of truth set out in Scripture.

Peter also warns of false teachers being present among believers. I urge you to read the whole of 2 Peter 2, but for now we will read the first two verses:

> "But there were false prophets also among the people, even as there shall be false teachers among you, who privily shall bring in damnable heresies, even denying the Lord that bought them and bring upon themselves swift destruction. And many shall follow their pernicious ways; by reason of whom the way of truth shall be evil spoken of."

Peter warns that these false teachers will be right there among professing Christians, spreading their evil teaching but making it sound plausible and attractive so that, as Peter says, many follow their ways. Interestingly, Peter goes on in 3:2 to instruct believers to be mindful of the *actual words* of the prophets and commandments of the Lord delivered through the apostles. Once again, this is an emphasis on the detailed words of those divinely-appointed messengers which should alone form the basis of what Christians believe and adhere to.

And if we were to look at the apostle John's writings we would see *his* voice added to this theme. In 1 John 4:1-6, John also warns that there are many false prophets and that what is said needs to be tested before being accepted. John gives a fundamental test by which we can determine whether what is being said derives from the

Spirit of truth or the spirit of error. In 4:2 he declares that

"Every spirit that confesseth that Jesus Christ is come in the flesh is of God."

John was very concerned to emphasise that the teaching concerning the person of Christ is vital and must be held at all cost. This fits well with the Gospel of John in which John portrays Jesus as the Son of God and reveals many distinctive truths about the person of Christ. Let all of us who are Christians take heed of John's instruction and beware of anyone of any position who tries to put forward anything contrary to Scripture as to who Christ is and what He has done!

Finally, in regard to this second phrase, I would like to draw your attention to one of the things which Paul had to say in his first letter to Timothy. In 1 Timothy 4:1, he writes that the Holy Spirit expressly warns that in these latter times some will depart from the faith through giving attention to seducing spirits and doctrines emanating from demons, compared with "the doctrine" mentioned in the last verse of that chapter. In verse 6 we see again the emphasis placed by the Holy Spirit on the knowledge of the *actual words* of the faith. In that verse, Timothy is urged to remind his fellow-believers of these important things, in effect passing on to them the flame of the truth to hold and to guard.

So, we have seen from these examples that Paul, Jude, Peter and John combine in the same theme that there is one, and only one, source of truth – the Holy Spirit through the divinely appointed prophets and apostles. We are warned to expect that that set of sound words will be under attack from satanic sources through individuals who may be within the church masquerading as true believers.

IN FAITH AND LOVE WHICH IS IN CHRIST JESUS

For our third phrase, let's consider very briefly the last few words of 2 Timothy 1:13 which tell us that we are to hold the sound words heard from the apostle "in faith and love which is in Christ Jesus." I suggest that these words tell us that we should hold this form or outline of sound words with a right spiritual attitude. Our belief is not in a theoretical or academic set of words or ideas. Our belief is in a living Person, Christ Jesus, and the truth connected with Him. We hold that belief first of all in a living *faith* in God and His Word and we then show and share our belief in *love* to those around us. This would stop us being legalistic about the truth. Yes, of course we stand firmly for the truth of Scripture and don't move on the fundamentals, but we display and discuss the truth in love, trying to carry on the pattern established by our Lord as recorded in John 1:17 where, in comparison with the legalism of the Old Testament times, it says that "grace and truth came by Jesus Christ."

HOLD FAST

I have deliberately left to fourth and final place the opening two words of our verse in 2 Timothy 1:13 where we are instructed to "Hold fast" this form of sound words received from the apostle. In the light of all that we have thought about already, here is a challenge to me and to you to *hold on to* that "outline of sound words" which each of us should have in our minds. That "outline of sound words" will not be magically imprinted on our minds and hearts. That will only come about by regular and careful *reading* of the Bible, day by day, and by *obedience* to it.

There is a thrilling record in Judges 7 of a battle where only 300 of God's earthly people, the Israelites, were up against a vastly bigger army of one of their enemies, the Midianites. The Israelites were led by Gideon who, like Timothy, had started off as a timid man. You can read of Gideon's battle plan from Judges 7:16-18. Let's now read verse 20 of that chapter:

> "And the three companies blew the trumpets, and brake the pitchers, and held the lamps in their left hands, and the trumpets in their right hands to blow withal: and they cried, The sword of the LORD, and of Gideon."

The verse tells us that in one hand they held a torch to throw light on the darkness around them. In the other hand, they held a trumpet to sound forth the noise of God's people. Part of their cry was "The sword of the LORD".

What a picture that is for God's people today! In Ephesians 6:17 it says that

> "the sword of the Spirit … is the word of God."

In Psalm 119:105 it is recorded that

> "Thy word is a lamp unto my feet, and a light unto my path."

Trumpets are often used in Scripture to convey the idea of God's message being sounded forth, for example in Numbers 10:1-10 and Revelation 1:10-11. As Gideon's army held on to these things, so we today are urged to hold on to what God has to say in His Word and to make His message clear to those around. In Gideon's day it brought a resounding victory. Today, as at any time in the church's history, it remains the only way for ultimate victory, however large and formidable the opposition may be.

At the end of 2 Timothy, in 4:3-4, Paul warned that a time would come when many would not tolerate sound and helpful instruction, wanting instead teaching which is appealing to their natural instincts and is easy to listen to – even if some of it is based on fables and not on God's Word. I firmly believe that that time has come and, as mentioned earlier, it is for every individual believer to seek to teach and adhere to the truth as set out in the Word of God even if some others, even in our churches, are not particularly interested in it.

What a temptation it is at times to change what the Bible actually says, perhaps to try to make the message sound more appealing or to try and make it fit better with changing social, political or moral views or standards. But that is not God's way, as we have seen from the verses which we have thought about today. To make such changes is to give in to the false teachers about whom we are warned.

At the small church which I attend, we have a few Christians in their teens and twenties. It is a great joy to see them grow in their knowledge and appreciation of the Word of God "which liveth and abideth for ever" (1 Peter 1:23). It is a responsibility but a privilege to pass on the torch to them and to pray that they might run faithfully with it, knowing and holding firmly to the pattern of sound words set out in the divinely inspired Bible.

Sanctification

SERIES: KEY BIBLE TEACHINGS

BROADCAST DATE: 11TH MARCH 2007

On the subject of *condemnation*, we have that wonderful statement in Romans 8:1:

> "There is therefore now no condemnation to them which are in Christ Jesus".

On the subject of *justification*, consider Romans 5:1:

> "Therefore being justified by faith, we have peace with God through our Lord Jesus Christ",

together with James 2:21, where justification by works is the outward evidence of what has taken place inside a person.

Our key subject here is *sanctification* – a word that is rarely used in day-to-day conversation but which is used frequently in both Old and New Testaments – a word that is applied to the Lord Jesus and to God's people and a word whose meaning is also the basic meaning of the related words *saint* and *sanctuary*.

Before going further into the details of sanctification, we should remind ourselves of a fundamental Bible principle which affects our subject. When God places someone into a particular position, that person's *right* to that position comes with God's authority and the position is not affected by that person's practical *response* in his or her living, although of course the life should match the position. For example, in the story of the prodigal son in Luke 15, the son was always his father's son. He behaved and lived in a completely inappropriate way but through it all his position as son remained the same, unaffected by his low level of practical living.

With that in mind, I would like to divide our subject into four aspects:

- positional sanctification;
- practical sanctification;
- sanctification applied to the Lord Jesus;
- the related words of saint and sanctuary.

POSITIONAL SANCTIFICATION

Let me use a simple illustration to try to help to convey the meaning of the word *sanctification*. Over the past few years, I have built up a modest collection of small model farm animals, mainly British breeds of cattle, pigs, sheep and horses. We all have our own interests and looking at these models gives me a lot of pleasure. No one else touches them. I decide how they are set out – they are set aside for my use and pleasure. Other people may or may not enjoy them, but I certainly do and they are there for me.

Sanctification means set apart for God's holy purpose or use. When God sanctifies someone or some people or some thing it means that He sets them or it apart from other people or other things so that they or it are there for His purpose and for the use of nobody else.

Now, let us spend a few minutes following through a few examples of this in the Bible. It is always useful to note the first reference in the Bible to any word or incident. The first reference to sanctification is in Genesis 2:3 where it says that

"God blessed the seventh day, and sanctified it".

That seventh day, the Old Testament Sabbath, was particularly set aside for God in Old Testament times as a reminder of God's rest, up to which God had been working in the first six days of creation. Subsequently God's Old Testament people had to keep that day holy as embodied in the fourth of the ten commandments recorded in Exodus 20.

In Exodus 19:10 & 14, it is said that all the Israelites were sanctified. As we read further through Exodus and Leviticus, we see that Aaron and his sons were sanctified as priests, that is set apart for God's purposes in that particular sphere of service for Him. In those two Bible books we also see references to particular objects being sanctified so that they are also separated for God's holy use, for example the altar, the tabernacle and the laver.

Perhaps it is worth pointing out that, in the Old Testament, the same Hebrew word may be translated *sanctify* or *consecrate* or *holy*. Similarly in the New Testament, in a number of cases in the Authorised Version of the Bible the words 'sanctification' and 'holiness' are simply different translations of the same Greek word.

When we come to the New Testament, there are two interesting references to sanctification in 1 Corinthians. Firstly, right at the beginning of the book, in 1:2, Paul addresses his letter to:

"the church of God which is at Corinth, to them that are sanctified in Christ Jesus".

Then in 6:11, after describing the nature of the unrighteous who would not inherit the kingdom of God, he goes on to say:

"And such were some of you: but ye are washed, but ye are sanctified".

These references are quite remarkable. The first letter to the Corinthians makes it very clear that many of the Christians at Corinth were anything but holy or righteous in their Christian living, but Paul emphasises right from the start of his letter that, *positionally* before God, they are sanctified because they are in Christ Jesus and have been made clean in Him. Incidentally, that washing has nothing to do with baptism but is because believers are sanctified with the blood of Jesus – see Hebrews 13:12. Our sanctification comes at great cost to God. In positional sanctification, the emphasis is on what is suitable in the view of God.

Let's read Hebrews 10:10 & 14:

"By the which will we are sanctified through the offering of the body of Jesus Christ once for all. ... For by one offering he hath perfected for ever them that are sanctified."

The letter to the Hebrews sets out a comparison between the things of the Old Testament and those of the New Testament, showing that the latter are better than the former. In the Old Testament, God desired Israel to be a nation set apart for Him, but they failed God and became often indistinguishable from the heathen nations. Now, in Hebrews, God shows that it is His will, His desire and decision, that a new people shall be set apart for Him and His pleasure. And how is this to be achieved? By the once-for-ever offering of the body of Jesus Christ.

From these verses in Hebrews chapter 10 we see the involvement of both Father and Son in sanctification. Now let's read part of 1 Peter 1:2:

> "Elect according to the foreknowledge of God the Father, through sanctification of the Spirit..."

So Peter tells us that the third Person of the Godhead, the Holy Spirit, is also involved in sanctification. If the Father's will determined sanctification and the offering of the Son is the basis of sanctification, then the Spirit is the divine Agent through whom sanctification is made real to us. Jesus said (John 3:6):

> "That which is born of the Spirit is spirit."

What a wonderful position is the position of being sanctified!

If in any doubt about the wonder of that position, let's read from Hebrews again, this time 2:11:

> "For both he that sanctifieth and they who are sanctified are all of one: for which cause he is not ashamed to call them brethren".

I will not even attempt to add to the wonder of those words!

So, that is the first area, the Bible truth of positional sanctification, a position into which God places me as soon as I become a born again Christian. It is not something which I increasingly move into as I grow as a Christian; I am placed once and for ever into that position which never changes.

PRACTICAL SANCTIFICATION

However, it is a different matter when we come to practical sanctification. There is no progress at all in positional sanctification. But in practical sanctification, the challenge to me is whether as a Christian I am *growing in holiness* as the years go by. In other words, is the way I live and behave increasingly appropriate to the position God has given me?

Take the example of King David in the Old Testament. He was chosen by God and placed by Him in a position as king and leader. Did David's behaviour match his position? Sadly, not always. Not long after the kingdom became fully his, David even committed adultery and murder. He wanted the beautiful woman Bathsheba for his wife but she was already married to a man called Uriah and King David arranged for Uriah to be placed in the front line in a fierce battle so that Uriah was killed and David could have Bathsheba. The sorry incident is recorded in 2 Samuel 11. Positionally, David remained king; practically, he often failed.

Earlier, we noted from Exodus 19 that all the nation of Israel were sanctified – that is in the positional sense of sanctification. Yet from time to time the people were told to sanctify themselves and be holy, for example in Leviticus 20:7. This is the idea of practical sanctification. Their way of living and their approach to God was to be consistent with their position as God's people. In their lives they were to demonstrate the fact that they were set apart for God's holy purpose, to live and behave differently from the nations around them. Sadly, they frequently failed. We only need to skim through the book of Numbers, which records the Israelites' journey from Mount Sinai to the River Jordan, to note examples of their constant failures. Regular practical failure there was, but positionally they remained God's people.

Let us follow through this idea of practical sanctification to a few verses in the New Testament, starting with John 17. This chapter contains intimate details of the Lord's prayer to His Father and in verse 16 Jesus says:

> "They are not of the world, even as I am not of the world."

Jesus stated the position of believers as belonging to another place. He then goes on to pray in verse 17:

> "Sanctify them through thy truth: thy word is truth."

The desire of Jesus was that believers who belonged to another place would be practically sanctified; that sanctification being achieved through the truth – as seen in and spoken by Jesus, the Son of God – that sets us apart from the world. How important it is then that I know that truth because, without it, I shall not be able to be practically sanctified.

In his first letter to the Thessalonian Christians, Paul makes two references to sanctification, both in the practical sense. First, in 4:3-4, he says:

> "For this is the will of God, even your sanctification, that ye should abstain from fornication: that every one of you should know how to possess his vessel in sanctification and honour".

In the first part of this chapter, Paul is laying great emphasis on the need for practical holiness. He states that this is God's will for us. In the world in which the Thessalonians lived, dominated by the Roman Empire, sexual impurity was the norm. Paul was instructing the Thessalonian Christians to be, and to be seen to be, separated from that way of unholy living which was against God's will and inappropriate for those whom God has sanctified. And let us note that God's standards never change and so sexual impurity is unacceptable for God's people today.

Secondly, in 1 Thessalonians 5:23, Paul writes:

"the very God of peace sanctify you wholly".

God, whose will it is that we should be practically sanctified, desires that that sanctification should be of my entire being, with no part of me unaffected, my "whole spirit and soul and body" as the verse goes on to say. Now that is some challenge for me! Am I completely sanctified, allowing the power of God to take control of every part of my being?

I wonder if at this stage I could briefly mention something which I have heard said occasionally over the years. The false logic goes along the lines that if I am saved and my position before God is secure and will not be altered, which is the case if genuinely I am born again, why worry about the way I live now? My position won't change, I will go to heaven anyway, so why go to the effort of seeking to live practically in a holy way? Paul deals with this important issue in Romans 6. Let's read verses 1-2:

"Shall we continue in sin, that grace may abound? God forbid. How shall we, that are dead to sin, live any longer therein?"

While there are a number of other references to practical sanctification in the New Testament, we will look at only one other. 2 Timothy 2:21 reads:

"If a man therefore purge himself from these, he shall be a vessel unto honour, sanctified, and meet for the master's use, and prepared unto every good work."

I understand that in the original language the word translated *purge* in this verse is a very strong one meaning 'to cleanse out'. What I learn from this verse is that if I want to be useful for the Lord, I myself have to make the effort to set myself apart from any thing or any association which leads to unholiness. Of course, I do this cleansing out through the power of the Spirit of God who dwells in me (see Romans 8:9) but I have to determine in my heart to do it.

SANCTIFICATION APPLIED TO THE LORD JESUS

I have in mind two scriptures in John's Gospel. The first is in 10:36, where it refers to

> "him, whom the Father hath sanctified, and sent into the world",

and the second is in 17:19, where Jesus says to His Father:

> "for their sakes I sanctify myself".

These are marvellous scriptures! In 10:36 Jesus is saying that the Father set apart the Son for what the Father had in mind and sent the Son into the world to carry out that purpose.

In 17:19 where Jesus says "for their sakes I sanctify myself", it could be that there are two further thoughts to bring out regarding Jesus's sanctification. One is that Jesus is the supreme Example of setting Himself apart for God, to achieve God's purpose and will. It is recorded in John 6:38 that Jesus said:

> "I came down from heaven, not to do mine own will, but the will of him that sent me."

Jesus was holy and He lived out perfectly that holiness in everything that He did and said, so much so that even one of the thieves crucified alongside Jesus could say (Luke 23:41):

> "We receive the due reward of our deeds: but this man hath done nothing amiss."

The writer to the Hebrews describes Jesus as

> "holy, harmless, undefiled, separate from sinners" (Hebrews 7:26).

So we see Jesus as the only perfect Person ever to live on this earth – indeed, the supreme Example of holy living! There is a verse of a hymn that comes to mind:

> *Saviour, we Thy path retrace,*
> *Patient love and lowly grace,*
> *Matchless, holy, all Thy ways;*
> *Saviour, we adore Thee.*

The second consideration in that statement "for their sakes I sanctify myself" is that Jesus is setting Himself apart in glory in heaven so that not only is He the supreme Example of holy living while He was on earth, but also He is in heaven for God and as our Object in glory. He has set Himself apart there so that the Holy Spirit can point us to the glory of Jesus in heaven, thereby sanctifying us today.

SAINT AND SANCTUARY

Finally, I would like briefly to refer to two other Bible words which have the same underlying meaning as sanctification, that is, set apart for God's holy purpose. One is the word *sanctuary*, frequently used in the Old Testament and also a few times in Hebrews. In the Old Testament, the sanctuary was a place set apart – a place distinct from other places – a place where, separated from others, God's glory and mind could be revealed. In Psalm 73, the writer sets out the problems and uncertainties of life which were too painful for him; but he then records in verse 17:

"Until I went into the sanctuary of God; then understood I their end."

The second related word is *saints*. Earlier, I quoted part of 1 Corinthians 1:2 and I would like now to quote more of that verse:

"Unto the church of God which is at Corinth, to them that are sanctified in Christ Jesus, called saints…".

In the New Testament, saints are holy ones, those set apart for God, belonging to God. It is God, not Paul or any other human being, who bestows on us this title. What dignity and standing this gives to believers! Paul used the term frequently in his writings and we need not shy away from using this lovely scriptural term. Let us also remember that there is a manner of behaviour, a way of living, which is appropriate to saints. On at least two occasions Paul uses the phrase "as becometh saints" – in Romans 16:2 and Ephesians 5:3.

What an extensive, wonderful and key subject *sanctification* is! Jesus the supreme Example, the marvellous, unchanging position in which God has placed every believer in Jesus, and the practical challenge of holy living which is consistent with our position!

The power for a minister – 2 Corinthians 12 and 13

SERIES: CHRISTIAN MINISTRY AND THE MINISTER

BROADCAST DATE: 3RD JUNE 2007

The topic of "Christian ministry and the minister" in Paul's second letter to the Corinthians can be considered under the following headings:

chapters 1-3	The *cost* of ministry;
chapters 4-5	The *motive* for ministry;
chapters 6-7	The *consequences* of ministry;
chapters 8-9	Ministry in *giving*;
chapters 10-11	The *marks* of a minister;
chapters 12-13	The *power* for a minister.

Our subject here is the last of these. Let's start by reading 2 Corinthians 12:9, a key verse in our section:

> "And he (that is, the Lord) said unto me, My grace is sufficient for thee: for my strength is made perfect in weakness. Most gladly therefore will I rather glory in my infirmities, that the power of Christ may rest upon me."

We see from this verse that the power for a minister, our subject, is the power of Christ Himself.

I would like to divide these two chapters into four sections.

12:1-4	Paul's vision;
12:5-18	Not Paul's abilities but Christ's power;
12:19 – 13:10	A warning;
13:11-14	The conclusion.

PAUL'S VISION (12:1-4)

The first four verses of chapter 12 say:

> "It is not expedient for me doubtless to glory. I will come to visions and revelations of the Lord. I knew a man in Christ above fourteen years ago, (whether in the body, I cannot tell; or whether out of the body, I cannot tell: God knoweth;) such an one caught up to the third heaven. And I knew such a man, (whether in the body, or out of the body, I cannot tell: God knoweth;) how that he was caught up into paradise, and heard unspeakable words, which it is not lawful for a man to utter."

While the beginning of verse 2 attributes the vision to an unnamed man in Christ, it is clear from verse 7 that that man is Paul himself. The wonder of this vision remained vividly with him 14 years after the event. In the vision, he was caught up to the third heaven, the highest place referred to in the Bible, to paradise, in the presence of God Himself. There he heard of things which human words cannot describe and even if they could, as a man Paul was not permitted to pass on these things to other men.

Paul never wants boastfully to draw attention to himself. That is one reason why he refers to the vision being given to the unnamed man in Christ. However, I suggest that there is another reason. Paul may well be wanting to draw attention to what is the position of any born again Christian, because every true believer, man or woman, is covered by the phrase "a man in Christ". In 1 Corinthians 15:44-50, Paul wrote about two races of people. The first race is Adam's race and every human being is born into that race. Like Adam, that race is *earthly*. But the second race is based on the Lord from heaven and every true believer is part of that *heavenly* race. Paul says in 2 Corinthians 5:17:

> "Therefore if any man be in Christ, he is a new creature (or, *creation*)".

So the man in Christ has access to great, heavenly things beyond the understanding of Adam's race. These things are not just available to the apostles, but to any man in Christ. My passport confirms that I am a British citizen. I am very happy to be a British citizen. But I am even happier to know that my new citizenship is in heaven and that gives me divine and eternal blessings which neither British nor any other earthly citizenship brings.

NOT PAUL'S ABILITIES BUT CHRIST'S POWER (12:5-18)

As Paul begins verse 1 of this chapter, so he continues in verse 5 that he does not glory or boast in himself but he will boast in his infirmities or weaknesses. What a strange thing to say!

In attempting to explain this, let us first of all read verses 7-8:

> "And lest I should be exalted above measure through the abundance of the revelations, there was given to me a thorn in the flesh, the messen-

ger of Satan to buffet me, lest I should be exalted above measure. For this thing I besought the Lord thrice, that it might depart from me."

Paul had been greatly privileged to hear the amazing things in his vision. In order for Paul not to become puffed up by these revelations, God gave him this "thorn in the flesh" to remind Paul constantly of his own limitations. We just don't know what disability comprised Paul's thorn in the flesh, but it was sent by God for this particular purpose and would not be pleasant – verse 7 uses the word 'buffet'. Amazingly, verse 7 also tells us that God used Satan to implement this thorn. What a wonderful Scripture to remind us that, while Satan's powers are great, he can only operate within limitations imposed by the all-powerful God! We can't understand why God permits Satan to have such powers but God is referred to in Ephesians 1:11 as

"him who worketh all things after the counsel of his own will".

It is interesting to note from verse 8 that as soon as Paul had this problem, he turned to prayer. This was not just a light prayer but a deep beseeching that the Lord might remove this problem. But it was not to be and Paul seemed to recognise this by only praying in this way three times. We can't help but think that the Lord also prayed in a deep beseeching way three times in the Garden of Gethsemane.

We now come to the key verse 9 which we read earlier and which begins:

"And he said unto me, My grace is sufficient for thee: for my strength is made perfect in weakness."

What lovely comforting words which come down the ages to all believers in whatever circumstances: "My grace is sufficient for thee"! As I came to this precise point in preparing this message, a dear Christian lady from the church I attend came to my door. She was scheduled to go into hospital the next day for an operation and I shared with her these comforting words from the Lord. Dear reader, if you feel that your circumstances are very trying, almost too hard to bear, these words of the Lord come to you in all their love and power: "My grace is sufficient for thee". He knows, He loves, He cares and no circumstance is beyond His wonderful grace.

For Paul the minister, the message was that this thorn was to continue. But if the thorn made Paul feel inadequate in his service, actually that was a good thing for it is in that recognition of my personal weakness, that Christ's strength comes in. So Paul boasted in his weaknesses because these in fact allowed the power of Christ to come in and take over. Someone else has paraphrased the last words of verse 9 as "that the strength and power of Christ may pitch a tent over me."

Here then, is the true power of a minister, be it Paul or someone today. If I rely on my own resources, my service for the Lord will fail. It is only through the power of the Christ of God that I can minister or serve to the glory of God. Is it the power of Christ, rather than of myself, that I am relying on for my service for Him?

Paul goes on in 12:10 to draw a conclusion from his argument. He had suffered many things as a minister of Christ, describing them in this verse as infirmities, reproaches, necessities, persecutions and distresses. But he had learned actually to take pleasure in these things because in those times of natural weakness when he couldn't rely on himself, he knew that he was relying solely on the power and strength of Christ, so that, at the end of verse 10, he makes the paradoxical statement:

"for when I am weak, then am I strong."

In the remainder of this second section, from verses 11-18, Paul is stressing that he truly is an apostle and has demonstrated the qualities of a true minister of Christ. And these attributes and qualities of an apostle and a minister had been demonstrated for 18 months in the very presence of the Corinthian Christians on Paul's first visit to them. They themselves had seen Paul perform the actions that indicate a genuine apostle, as outlined in verse 12 of our chapter – patience, signs, wonders and mighty deeds.

In these verses 12:11-18, Paul also draws our attention to some of the qualities which ought to be seen in a minister of Christ.

- He did not want to be burdensome to them by taking from them (verses 13, 14 & 16).
- He did not craftily use any who assisted him indirectly to gain from them (verses 16-18).
- He sought to care and provide for them like a spiritual parent (verse 14).
- He was willing to go to the very limit of his energy to benefit them (verse 15).
- He continued to love them, and love them abundantly, even when his love was not returned (verse 15).

Please note these qualities of a true minister of Christ; these same qualities ought to be seen in every servant of Christ today. I find this a great challenge. And please also note that these qualities were demonstrated consistently over an extended period of time right in Corinth where these Christians lived. Paul wasn't just a man who talked about principles; what he said, he lived out! What a commendation it is when a minister or a servant of Christ today really does live out what he or she says, through the power of Christ!

A WARNING (12:19 – 13:10)

Some of the Christians in the church at Corinth had a strained relationship with Paul. I deliberately say that the strain in the relationship was from the side of the Corinthians. As far as Paul was concerned, he loved all the Christians at Corinth but that did not stop Paul from speaking out clearly on the truth of God and the sort of practical living which ought to be seen in Christians. Some of the Christians at Corinth did not like such straight talking and so sought to question Paul's authority as an apostle. Paul as a true minister or servant did not stop loving them, but equally did not stop speaking out when anything fell short of God's truth or standards.

We need to recognise that the apostles of New Testament times had the authority to discipline individuals. For example, in 13:10 the apostle Paul refers to "the power which the Lord hath given me". Notice that this authority comes from "the Lord", the title used when Jesus is being presented as the One with supreme authority. This final message from Paul to the Corinthians, before he concludes his letter to them, is a message of solemn warning, backed by his divinely-given authority as an apostle.

It seems to me that the verses in this section contain some important guidance on applying corrective action in a church today. First let's read 12:19:

"Again, think ye that we excuse ourselves unto you? we speak before God in Christ: but we do all things, dearly beloved, for your edifying."

There are at least three matters of guidance in this verse.

1. Any corrective action is conducted *before God*, in the right manner and in the light of God's word. This means also that the motives for the correction are righteous ones which stand up in the sight of God.

2. The corrective action is carried out *in a loving way*. Before going into his serious warning, Paul addresses all of them in this verse as "dearly beloved". There is a fine balance between dealing adequately with a problem and yet not being legalistic as the Pharisees were.

3. The aim of correction ultimately is *edifying* or building up. This is reinforced at the end of 13:10 where Paul says that the power was given to him "to edification, and not to destruction". Taking corrective action in the appropriate manner builds up the church by dealing with sin and also aims to build up the one or ones being corrected, by urging repentance and ultimate restoration of fellowship with the church.

Paul is telling these Corinthian Christians that they all need to repent and abandon the sinful practices which had marked some of them and he urges them to do it in response to this letter. Otherwise he warns that he will have to address the problem on his next visit to them and will have to use the sharpness of his authority referred to in 13:10. Paul would much rather consider positive matters on the occasion of his visit, but if he has to address their poor state of Christian living he will not hesitate to do so. It was not the way of Paul to avoid any issue or to sweep anything under the carpet. As he writes in 13:2:

"... I write to them which heretofore have sinned, and to all other, that, if I come again, I will not spare".

The two categories of the Corinthians' failings which were troubling Paul are outlined in 12:20-21. The first category in verse 20 contained sins such as envyings, strifes and backbitings and had to do with their *self-will*. The second category in verse 21 were more to do with the misuse of the body, sins such as uncleanness and fornication, and had to do with their *self-indulgence*.

The second sentence of 13:1 reads:

"In the mouth of two or three witnesses shall every word be established."

If Paul visited Corinth again and an accusation was raised against a particular Christian, Paul would require *more than one witness* to support the accusation. This principle was established by God in Old Testament times, for example in Deuteronomy 19:15, and is specifically carried forward into the church period. A further example is in 1 Timothy 5:19 which reads:

"Against an elder receive not an accusation, but before two or three witnesses."

We do well to follow that principle today.

Verse 9 reads:

"For we are glad, when we are weak, and ye are strong: and this also we wish, even your perfection."

It is another statement of Paul's ambition as a minister of Christ. His desire was not for himself, but for the strengthening of the believers in Corinth whom he was serving. He wanted and prayed for them to grow spiritually so that they were maturing in Christian things. More lessons for ministers of Christ today! Those we serve should be more important to us than ourselves and should be in our prayers, desiring spiritual progress for them.

So, this third section is a solemn one, containing a warning to these Christians in Corinth who were erring. At the same time it is interesting to note the lessons in it for ministers of Christ today and for handling the always difficult matters of correction.

THE CONCLUSION (13:11-14)

In this second letter to the Corinthians Paul has had to confront a number of issues relating to inappropriate behaviour and attitudes amongst some of the church at Corinth. No issue has been avoided and there has been some straight speaking which must have hit the consciences of those believers who needed to change their ways. Now in these last words of the letter, this minister of Christ desires to finish on an uplifting note and again there are lessons which we can learn.

Let's read verses 11–13:

> "Finally, brethren, farewell. Be perfect, be of good comfort, be of one mind, live in peace; and the God of love and peace shall be with you. Greet one another with an holy kiss. All the saints salute you."

Paul starts by calling them brethren. Whatever the faults and difficulties, he and they remained united by this lovely Bible term, brethren. Nothing he has had to say breaks that unity and he wants to convey to them the warmth of his feelings for them. He then tells them to face up to the challenges, to operate as mature Christians, to encourage and comfort each other. If they do these things, the very God of love and peace will be with them. It isn't that God was not with His people in Corinth, but if they themselves were not living together in the way Paul instructs, they could not enjoy the presence of the God who is the author of love and peace.

In verse 13, he conveys to them the salutations of all the saints, all the believers where Paul was when he wrote this letter. What a tremendous thing to know that there are links of affection across the world between all believers, whether we have met them or not. And the salutations were from *all* the believers, again emphasising that the problems at Corinth did not stop all believers from uniting in their love for each other.

Finally, we come to the last verse, verse 14. What a great verse, used by many believers over the years! It is one of the verses which demonstrates the truth of the teaching on the Trinity. We often refer to God the Father, Son and Holy Spirit and that may well be the order most often used in the New Testament. But in this verse, the order is Son, Father and Holy Spirit. Perhaps the grace of our Lord Jesus Christ comes first because it is that grace, the undeserved favour of the Lord Jesus Christ, which the Corinthians, in all their needs, had to be aware of first, before they could appreciate the love of God and then enjoy the fellowship of the Holy Spirit. If the Corinthians really thought about this verse when they read it, they would be both humbled and encouraged that Divine Persons were bestowing such favours on them.

At the end of our study on 2 Corinthians 12 and 13, I can't do better than quote this final verse:

> "The grace of the Lord Jesus Christ, and the love of God, and the communion of the Holy Ghost, be with you all. Amen."

Jonathan

SERIES: MEN WHO MET DAVID

BROADCAST DATE: 23RD SEPTEMBER 2007

One of the men who met David was the infamous Goliath in that thrilling story in 1 Samuel 17 where the young lad David, with apparently little protection and no hope, met the giant Goliath in a one-to-one duel and defeated and killed the giant. David had the protection of God's strength which was all that he needed.

That meeting with David was a one-off and a fight. The meeting for our subject could not be more different! This time, the man who met David is Jonathan, a prince meeting a shepherd boy, but the two of them became the best of friends. It is a lovely story but I also find it one of the saddest stories in the Bible, as we shall see.

BACKGROUND TO THE FRIENDSHIP

In Samuel's advancing years, and given the corruption of his sons, the elders of Israel came to Samuel and asked for a king to rule over them, just like all the other nations round about (1 Samuel 8:1-6). God told Samuel to go along with this request, even though effectively it meant that Israel had rejected God. Saul was then chosen as king and he seemed ideal for the position, being from a well-off background, a handsome young man and an imposing figure, much taller than anyone else. Saul started off well, winning victories over Israel's enemies. But it wasn't long before Saul's faults became evident. He started disobeying God and ignoring the words of Samuel, God's messenger. Saul's downward path is a sobering record in the first book of Samuel. The lesson is that the outward appearance is irrelevant in working for God. Saul seemed to have everything to make him a success but, crucially, his heart was not right before God.

God's people, Israel, had many enemies and 1 Samuel particularly records the constant battles between Israel and the Philistines; but in trying to do things in his own strength Saul failed and eventually the Philistines killed him, as recorded in 1 Samuel 31. It was against this background of Saul's failure that God acted to choose a person who would replace Saul as king, "a man after his (the LORD's) own heart" (1 Samuel 13:14). That man was David – see 1 Samuel 16.

This is what makes this friendship between David and Jonathan so remarkable. Jonathan was the oldest son of Saul and should himself have succeeded to the throne of Israel. But Jonathan saw qualities in God's man, David, which led Jonathan to love, protect and promote David. I should add that there are a number of other Jonathans in the Bible but none is covered extensively.

With that background, we will now look into some of the detail. The events of the life of Jonathan are recorded in many of the chapters in 1 Samuel, from chapter 13 to chapter 31. I would like us to consider some of those events and to think of the lessons which we might draw from them as we proceed through the chapters. I want to do this bearing in mind that in a number of ways David can be taken as a picture, or *type*, of the Lord Jesus. As already mentioned, David was a man after God's own heart. David was introduced from a humble background, but became king. For many years, David was hated by the leaders of his day and rejected by many of the people, including his own brothers, but there were some who saw that David was God's man and who were willing to follow him and join in his rejection. These are just a few of the parallels with what happened to Jesus which allow us to accept that, in some ways, David is a type of the Lord Jesus. Of course, all Old Testament types fall short of the reality and Jesus far exceeds anything David was or did.

BACKGROUND CLUES TO JONATHAN'S CHARACTER

Jonathan is first mentioned in 1 Samuel 13 and I would like us initially to look at the events concerning him in chapters 13 and 14. This is before the recorded first meeting between David and Jonathan in chapter 18 and so chapters 13 and 14 are providing us with some background clues as to the character of Jonathan, particularly in comparison with his father, King Saul, who, even in these early days of his being king, was displaying many worrying features.

Saul takes credit for Jonathan's victory

Note first of all the *problems* that emerge from Saul's nature and actions and, secondly, the *benefits* that come from Jonathan's character and actions. The first comparison is in 13:1-4, which reads:

> "Saul reigned one year; and when he had reigned two years over Israel, Saul chose him three thousand men of Israel; whereof two thousand were

with Saul in Michmash and in mount Bethel, and a thousand were with Jonathan in Gibeah of Benjamin: and the rest of the people he sent every man to his tent. And Jonathan smote the garrison of the Philistines that was in Geba, and the Philistines heard of it. And Saul blew the trumpet throughout all the land, saying, Let the Hebrews hear. And all Israel heard say that Saul had smitten a garrison of the Philistines, and that Israel also was had in abomination with the Philistines. And the people were called together after Saul to Gilgal."

From these four verses we note that it was Jonathan with his smaller army who actually won the victory over the Philistines, although Saul took the credit and drew attention to it by blowing a trumpet and boasting of the victory as if it was his. Jonathan quietly got on with the job, even though someone else hijacked the publicity.

Saul fails, but Jonathan achieves things for God

The rest of chapter 13 makes sorry reading. After Jonathan's victory, the Philistines put together a large force to make battle against Israel and the Israelites with Saul were scared stiff, hiding in caves and some even leaving Canaan. Then Saul makes a massive mistake, displaying his impatience and lack of appreciation of the reality of God's word. He takes the place of a priest and makes a burnt offering so that God speaks to him through Samuel in verses 13-14:

"Thou hast done foolishly: thou hast not kept the commandment of the LORD thy God, which he commanded thee: for now would the LORD have established thy kingdom upon Israel for ever. But now thy kingdom shall not continue..."

Saul was all about himself and any notion of obeying and serving God was superficial. Chapter 13 ends with the painting of a bleak picture: the Israelites under Saul had very few weapons to fight against the large Philistine army which was advancing against them.

Then, in the first verse of chapter 14, Jonathan takes the initiative. With only his armour bearer, he moves out, without telling his father, to take the fight to the enemy. All sorts of obstacles face him including problems in his journey (verses 4-5), but in faith in God he utters the words in verse 6:

> "Come, and let us go over unto the garrison of these uncircumcised: it may be that the LORD will work for us: for there is no restraint to the LORD to save by many or by few."

Jonathan's armour bearer grew in faith and joined in the fight as he followed Jonathan's example. The two of them killed 20 Philistines causing the whole of the Philistine army to tremble.

Meanwhile, Saul unwisely had instructed all of his army to refrain from eating and they were not happy about this. Jonathan, unaware of Saul's ruling, ate some wild honey. Saul found out and was determined that Jonathan must die. But the Israelites had a high estimation of Jonathan who had so encouraged them and they would not allow Saul to kill him. Chapter 14 closes with Saul continuing to look only on outward appearances by seeking to recruit for his army any man who seemed to be big and strong. Saul had still not learned the lesson of trusting God for victory by whatever means God chose.

So, chapters 13 and 14 show us Saul looking to enhance himself but not having true faith and not truly submitting to what God had to say. With Saul it was all about outward appearances. In comparison, Jonathan achieves things for God, recognising that salvation and victory come from God. He doesn't draw attention to himself and gives encouragement to individuals and to the whole nation of Israel, God's earthly people. His is real faith in action, not in words only! There, in those far-gone days of about 3,000 years ago, are some lessons which I can take hold of today.

Saul fails, and David appears

After those initial incidents in the life of Jonathan in 1 Samuel 13 and 14, we don't read of him again until chapter 18. In the intervening chapters, chapter 15 demonstrates more of Saul's inadequacies but, crucially, chapters 16 and 17 introduce us to David, God's choice as a replacement for the failed first king. David, the youngest son and apparently the least expected of Jesse's sons to be king, was in fact God's choice. God saw in David what He did not see in any other; just as, nearly a thousand years later, God saw qualities in Jesus when all others around were failures. In chapter 17 there is the battle of David versus Goliath, and so David emerges as God's choice and as the rescuer of Israel.

JONATHAN MEETS DAVID

Now we come to chapter 18 where Jonathan has heard David speak for the first time and there is an immediate bond between the two of them. 18:1 & 3-4 read:

> "And it came to pass, when David had made an end of speaking unto Saul, that the soul of Jonathan was knit with the soul of David, and Jonathan loved him as his own soul. ... Then Jonathan and David made a covenant, because he loved him as his own soul. And Jonathan stripped himself of the robe that was upon him, and gave it

to David, and his garments, even to his sword, and
to his bow, and to his girdle."

A few words from David, and Jonathan's whole being –
his very soul – responded to David. Look forward to the
Gospels and we hear the words of Jesus to some fishermen: "Follow Me" (Matthew 4:19). And immediately
those fishermen left their nets to follow Jesus! What a
great moment it is when any one of us recognises the
beauty and greatness of Jesus and gives our whole being
to Him. Isaac Watts wrote:

> *Love so amazing, so divine,*
> *Demands my soul, my life, my all.*

That is the basis of becoming a Christian. It is not just a
formal recognition of who Jesus is, but an appreciation
of Him in our souls and the formation of a personal
relationship with Him, as there was between Jonathan
and David (1 Samuel 18:1).

Jonathan the prince also recognised that David, this
young shepherd lad, was in fact greater than himself.
And so in verse 4 Jonathan gives to David his garments,
his weapons and his belt; that is, everything that spoke
of his own position and achievements. In my life I have
to own the superiority of Jesus and that my victory and
strength can only come from Him. The remainder of
chapter 18 concerns firstly the continuing advancement
of David, perhaps summed up in verse 14:

> "David behaved himself wisely in all his ways; and
> the Lord was with him",

and secondly Saul's jealousy of David and Saul's false
motives in his actions.

JONATHAN STANDS UP FOR DAVID

In chapter 19, Saul's hatred and jealousy of David deepen and he plots to kill David. Verse 2 says that "Jonathan … delighted much in David" and he tried to reason with his father by pointing out the good that was in David, by emphasising that David had shown no enmity to Saul and by recounting the exploits of David which had brought benefits to Israel. Saul temporarily relented of his intention to kill David, but very quickly returned to his determination to get rid of him.

Yet again we see Jonathan being true to David and indeed being brave enough to stand up for him in front of the king. Make no mistake about it, this action could have cost Jonathan his life! I am challenged about my own bravery to stand up for Jesus when others, sometimes powerful, influential people who could cause me problems, are showing that they despise or even hate my Saviour.

I don't want to omit consideration of that phrase from verse 2:

"Jonathan … delighted much in David".

Thinking of the qualities of David would bring great pleasure to Jonathan. I remember as a boy that I would often find my father sitting with his Bible open and meditating on the Lord Jesus. The Amplified Version of the Bible (AMP) expresses the first few words of Psalm 45 as:

"My heart overflows with a goodly theme".

Do I spend enough time delighting in Jesus so that, as I increasingly appreciate Him, my heart overflows? This is the picture I get from Jonathan's considerations of David.

JONATHAN'S COMMITMENT TO DAVID

In the first verse of chapter 20, Saul's plotting causes David to flee for his life. David, though innocent of seeking any harm to Saul, is being persecuted by him. How like Jesus, who sinned against no one but was nevertheless hated by so many!

Jonathan's commitment to David is summed up in 20:4 when he says:

> "Whatsoever thy soul desireth, I will even do it for thee."

Jonathan wanted to perform whatever it was that David wanted. I ask myself, is that my desire for Jesus?

David and Jonathan agree that Jonathan will find out whether it is safe for David to return into Saul's presence and they devise a means of transmitting the answer to that question. The message was to be transmitted through archery. David was to hide himself at an agreed spot and Jonathan, with a servant, would take his bow and fire three arrows. The servant would then be sent to find the arrows. If Jonathan called to the servant that the arrows were on this side of him, the message was that all was well for David to return. On the other hand, if Jonathan called that the arrows were beyond the servant, David would have to leave because Saul's anger against him was unchanged. Sadly, the message was that the arrows were beyond the servant boy. The boy was sent away and David and Jonathan parted as recorded in the last two verses of chapter 20:

> "... they kissed one another, and wept with one another, until David exceeded. And Jonathan said to David, Go in peace, forasmuch as we have sworn both of us in the name of the LORD, saying,

The LORD be between me and thee, and between my seed and thy seed for ever. And he arose and departed: and Jonathan went into the city."

JONATHAN LEAVES DAVID

Here, then, was the parting of the ways. David leaves and the remaining chapters of 1 Samuel largely deal with the period of David's rejection when he was hunted by Saul and his men like "a partridge in the mountains" (26:20). There was no doubt that Jonathan loved David and continued to do so to the very end. But Jonathan returned to the city (20:42). He was not willing to take his place with a rejected David. Instead, his loyalty to his father, Saul, took him back to the city when he should have been at the side of the one whom God had chosen.

What does this mean for me as a Christian today? At the cross, the world rejected Jesus. They said:

"Away with this man, ... Crucify him" (Luke 23:18 & 21).

I don't believe that that verdict on Jesus is any different today. Am I willing to take my place with a rejected Jesus, whatever the cost? The cost may be significant in terms of difficulties with family or friends or colleagues or career. This is such a sad point in the life of Jonathan. His love for, and loyalty to David were great but he was not willing to be rejected with David.

JONATHAN ENCOURAGES DAVID

I think I am right in saying that there is only one other recorded meeting between David and Jonathan which is in 1 Samuel 23:16-18. They meet in a wood where David was hiding. The Bible beautifully records that Jonathan actually encouraged David and affirmed that David would become king of Israel. But these verses end with

David staying in the wood, the place of rejection, and Jonathan not staying with him but returning to his house.

THE DEATH OF JONATHAN

The death of Jonathan is recorded in 1 Samuel 31:1-2. He died in battle at his father's side at the hands of the Philistines. Jonathan stayed with his father and perished with him!

David's touching reaction to the news of the death of Saul and Jonathan is noted in 2 Samuel 1:17-27. We will read verses 23 & 25-26:

> "Saul and Jonathan were lovely and pleasant in their lives, and in their death they were not divided: they were swifter than eagles, they were stronger than lions. ... How are the mighty fallen in the midst of the battle! O Jonathan, thou wast slain in thine high places. I am distressed for thee, my brother Jonathan: very pleasant hast thou been unto me: thy love to me was wonderful, passing the love of women."

Obviously, these were words wrung from the heart of a deeply distressed David who had so valued his bond with Jonathan. Later we read in 2 Samuel 21:12-14 that David retrieved the bones of Saul and Jonathan and buried them in their family grave in the country of Benjamin.

IN CONCLUSION

I have followed through the life of Jonathan and sought to draw lessons for us from his life, particularly in his relationship with David, a picture of our relationship with the Lord Jesus. I should mention, without developing the idea, that Jonathan is also sometimes looked on as a picture of the future remnant of the Jews who, having left Jesus, the true David, will go through the Great Tribulation.

I trust that this lovely, touching story of Jonathan, who had so many of the qualities of faith, will be challenging to all Christians readers. The sad end to his story, when he was not willing to be with the rejected David, should challenge each of us as to our personal commitment to the Lord Jesus in our day, the day of His rejection.

Mark 4

Mark's Gospel presents Jesus as the *Servant* compared with Jesus as *King* in Matthew, as the *Son of Man* in Luke and as the *Son of God* in John. Mark's is the shortest of the four Gospels as things move quickly, in keeping with the constant action of a servant and the frequent use of words such as "straightway" and "immediately". It is noteworthy that, at least in the Authorised Version of the Bible, most of the chapters begin with the word "And", as though to emphasise that the life of Jesus was one continuous work of service. Unlike the other Gospels, there is no earthly or heavenly genealogy in Mark because the test of a servant is not his background but his ability actually to do the job well. It is also remarkable that the Holy Spirit chose Mark to write this Gospel about the perfect Servant, Jesus, when Mark himself failed in his early years of service for God – see Acts 13:13 and 15:37-38.

Mark 1 introduces Jesus, emphasising that, though a Servant, He is the Son of God. In verse 1 Mark mentions the *gospel*, that is the good news, a term used more frequently in Mark than the other three Gospels. The remainder of the first three chapters deal mainly with the call of the twelve disciples and a number of miracles.

Now we come to chapter 4. Mark's Gospel contains far more miracles than parables – more actions than words – in keeping with this presentation of Jesus as a Servant. Four of the relatively few parables in Mark are contained in this chapter, and, with a miracle, chapter 4 breaks down neatly into five parts:

verses 1-20	the parable of the sower;
verses 21-25	the parable of the candle or lamp;
verses 26-29	the parable of the secret growth of a seed;
verses 30-34	the parable of the mustard seed;
verses 35-41	the miracle where Jesus calms the storm on the lake.

THE PARABLE OF THE SOWER (VERSES 1-20)

First of all, then, the parable of the sower which Jesus tells in verses 1-9 and explains in verses 10-20. This parable and its explanation are also recorded in Matthew 13 and Luke 8, with slight changes of emphasis. The story was one to which all the listeners could relate. It would be a common sight to see a farmer spreading seed by hand. Inevitably, as he threw the seed out, it would fall on different sorts of ground with differing results. Jesus mentions four types of ground in His parable. First of all in verse 4 there is the *way side* or the *pathway*, uncultivated land where the birds came and ate the seed which just lay on the hard surface. Then some seed landed on *stony ground* with very shallow soil. The seed sprouted but as soon as the sun rose the fragile plants withered away because there was not sufficient soil for strong roots to form. Thirdly, in verse 7, some of the seed fell *among thorns* which were far stronger than the seedlings which the farmer wanted and those seedlings were smothered by the thorns. Lastly, in verse 8, some seed did fall on *good ground* and there was fruit of varying yields for the sower.

Now let's read verses 9-12 of our chapter:

"And he (Jesus) said unto them, He that hath ears to hear, let him hear. And when he was alone, they that were about him with the twelve asked of him the parable. And he said unto them, Unto you it is given to know the mystery of the kingdom of God: but unto them that are without, all these things are done in parables: that seeing they may see, and not perceive; and hearing they may hear, and not understand; lest at any time they should be converted, and their sins should be forgiven them."

The parable had been spoken by Jesus from a boat to the whole crowd gathered at the lakeside. To them, in verse 9, Jesus indicates that only some of the individuals in the crowd will have the spiritual ability really to hear and understand what is the spiritual message of these parables. Jesus explains this further to His disciples in verses 10-12. In the Bible, a *mystery* is something not revealed previously but now shown by God to those who are His own, those who have really heard and accepted His word. But those who are "without", to use the word in verse 11, that is those who don't belong to God, they look but they don't see, they hear but they don't understand and the parables of Jesus to them are merely interesting stories without conveying the underlying spiritual message.

There is a basic if unpopular principle here for Christians today: we can't expect people who are not born again Christians to understand the truth of God as set out in the Bible. Only those who have the Holy Spirit, that is all Christians, have the capacity to understand the things of God – as Jesus said in John 16:13:

"Howbeit when he, the Spirit of truth, is come, he will guide you into all truth: …"

So, the explanation of the parable was not offered by Jesus to the crowd but only to the twelve disciples and some others who remained with them. That explanation begins with the statement in verse 14:

"The sower soweth the word."

You may find it interesting to note the different introductions to the explanations of the parable of the sower. In Matthew 13:18 the emphasis is on the *sower*, it is "the parable of the sower." In Luke 8:11 the explanation begins with "The seed is the word of God", the emphasis being on the *seed*. Here in Mark 4:14 the act of *sowing* is emphasised, consistent with Jesus being presented as the Servant working at sowing.

Jesus goes on in verses 15-20 to explain what meaning there is in the four types of ground on which the seed fell. The way side or pathway tells us that the seed doesn't sink into the ground and, like the birds, as soon as the seed is sown Satan comes and takes it away. The stony ground is a picture of people who initially receive the word of God gladly but as soon as adverse conditions such as opposition arise, there is no root and so those people are upset and fall away. Thirdly, the people represented by the thorny ground are those who hear the word of God but the cares of the world and the desire for other things creep in and suffocate the word of God so that there is no fruit. Thankfully, there is a fourth ground, the good ground in verse 20 where the seed, the word of God, is genuinely received and welcomed, resulting in fruit for God.

This is a solemn parable because it tells us that most who hear the word of God do not really receive it. Most hearers are either hard hearted and indifferent, or shallow with no depth to their response, or are so preoccupied with worldly things that the word of God is choked out. Dear reader, I do hope that you are among those represented by the good ground because you have genuinely received God's word into your heart by taking Jesus as your Saviour and Lord. But even in the good ground we note that the seed brought varying levels of fruit for the sower. There is a challenge here for every Christian: am I totally committed to the Lord Jesus in my heart and life so that there is the maximum fruit for God? I suggest that fruit for God means becoming more like Jesus. In the context of Mark's Gospel, this would involve being wholehearted and ceaseless in my service for Him.

It is important to see how fundamental this parable of the sower is. In Matthew 13 it is the first of seven parables dealing with the kingdom of heaven. In Mark 4 it is the first parable in a chapter containing four parables in a Gospel which has relatively few parables. In Luke 8 it occupies a prominent position and is far more detailed than any of the parables previously recorded by Luke. It is one of the relatively few parables recorded in all three of what are often called the *synoptic* Gospels, that is Matthew, Mark and Luke.

In Matthew and Mark the parable of the sower follows immediately after the statement by Jesus as to His new relationships. No longer would His brethren be those with whom He had natural links, such as Mary His mother or the Jewish nation, but His brethren would be those with whom He had spiritual ties. Having stated that, as recorded in the last five verses of Mark 3, Jesus immediately goes on to tell this parable of the sower which emphasises that that new relationship comes about by hearing and receiving the seed, the word of God. Anything and everything else of a spiritual nature flows from that fact, which is why this parable is so important. God's kingdom grows through the spreading of the word.

THE PARABLE OF THE CANDLE (VERSES 21-25)

The second part of Mark 4 is verses 21-25:

> "And he said unto them, Is a candle brought to be put under a bushel, or under a bed? and not to be set on a candlestick? For there is nothing hid, which shall not be manifested; neither was any thing kept secret, but that it should come abroad. If any man have ears to hear, let him hear. And he said unto them, Take heed what ye hear: with what measure ye mete, it shall be measured to you: and unto you that hear shall more be given. For he that hath, to him shall be given: and he that hath not, from him shall be taken even that which he hath."

In this parable of the candle, I suggest that Jesus is emphasising two matters. First of all, receiving the seed, the word of God, not only produces *fruit* but also *light*. In John 9, one of the great Bible chapters about bringing light, Jesus miraculously gives sight to a man who had been blind since he was born. In John 9:5, Jesus says:

> "… I am the light of the world."

When the previously blind man was questioned by people, he could not provide all the answers but he was certain of something, as recorded in verse 25:

"... one thing I know, that, whereas I was blind, now I see."

The evidence of his dramatic change could be seen by everyone. Psalm 119:130 says:

"The entrance of thy words giveth light; it giveth understanding unto the simple."

So, receiving the word of God enables me to see and understand spiritual things which previously were hidden to me and in the dark, so to speak.

This parable of the candle also emphasises a second point. *Light isn't much use if it is hidden.* As Jesus said, a candle isn't brought to be put under a bowl or hidden under a bed but to put on a candlestick so that its light is seen and is of use. If I really have received the word of God then my light should be evident at home, at college, at work and to my friends and neighbours. Certainly in the context of Mark's Gospel, my service for God should be seen. Not that any Christian should be seeking to impress people with his or her service for God, but that service, conducted for God's glory and not mine, should be visible to all.

Again, there is the challenge in verse 23 to have ears that really do hear what Jesus is saying. However, in this case Jesus goes on in verses 24-25 to warn those listening then, and us today, to be careful what we are hearing. If we listen to the truth of the Bible we will gain in spiritual understanding and be able to understand even more. But if we listen to anything other than that truth, what little of spiritual things we do know even that will be damaged and effectively taken away from us.

THE PARABLE OF THE SECRET GROWTH OF A SEED (VERSES 26-29)

The third part of Mark 4 concerns the secret growth of a seed. To summarise the verses, they say that if a farmer who sows seed goes regularly, night and day, to see it, he doesn't know how the seed sprouts and grows and fruits. It just does! Then, eventually, the grain is ripe and the farmer sends in the harvesters. Jesus said that this is like the kingdom of God where the Lord's workers may and should work hard in sowing and caring, but the kingdom grows only through Divine influence, unseen by natural eyes.

The words of these verses 26-29 are recorded only in Mark and therefore need to be considered in the context of the theme of this book. Jesus is the Divine Sower and Reaper. However, I believe that there is also an acceptable application of these verses whereby, if my service for God is modelled on that of the perfect Servant, Jesus, it is right that I, like Jesus, should labour hard in the sowing of the seed, the word of God. However, real spiritual growth in hearts comes from an unseen Source which I can't influence. It is the work here of the Holy Spirit.

I am reminded of Psalm 126:5-6:

> "They that sow in tears shall reap in joy. He that goeth forth and weepeth, bearing precious seed, shall doubtless come again with rejoicing, bringing his sheaves with him."

THE PARABLE OF THE MUSTARD SEED (VERSES 30-34)

In the fourth section of the chapter, Jesus tells the parable of the mustard seed. Verses 31-32 read:

> "It (the kingdom of God) is like a grain of mustard seed, which, when it is sown in the earth, is less

than all the seeds that be in the earth: but when it is sown, it groweth up, and becometh greater than all herbs, and shooteth out great branches; so that the fowls of the air may lodge under the shadow of it."

This parable contains a warning for us. A tiny mustard seed is shown to grow into a great plant with great branches so that birds take shelter in it. The previous section of this chapter emphasised the Divine Source of the secret growth that takes place in the kingdom of God, the secret, real internal growth. In the parable of the mustard seed, the emphasis seems to be on the external, impressive growth which is clearly visible to all. Part of the clue in interpreting this must be in the statement in verse 32:

"… that the fowls of the air may lodge under the shadow of it."

In verses 4 & 15 of our chapter, it is stated that the fowls of the air represent Satan and it is consistent to carry that interpretation into the parable of the mustard seed.

This external aspect of the kingdom of God includes the influence of Satan and is therefore false and dangerous. It suggests to me something purporting to be the kingdom of God, something big and impressive but not real. Men have built a structure for the church which seems impressive but which actually contains not just true believers, but also those who are professing but not real believers. That structure is actually under the influence of Satan who wants to divert attention away from the truth, based solely on Jesus Christ who is the truth (John 14:6), to a big structure which actually has extended things beyond the word of God. What a solemn warning for the servants of God!

THE MIRACLE WHERE JESUS CALMS THE STORM ON THE LAKE (VERSES 35-41)

Finally in this chapter of parables, we come to the amazing miracle recorded in verses 35-41. After an exhausting day of talking to the crowds and to His followers, Jesus is taken by His disciples across the lake. Jesus falls asleep in the back of the boat, leaning on a pillow, the only time in Mark's Gospel where the perfect Servant is recorded as sleeping. The lake was susceptible to sudden storms arising and in the words of verse 37:

"... there arose a great storm of wind, and the waves beat into the ship, so that it was now full."

The disciples, some of them fishermen experienced in the storms of Lake Galilee, were concerned for their own safety and awoke Jesus, who rebuked the wind and said only three words to the sea, "Peace, be still." From the "great storm" of verse 37 there was the transformation to a "great calm" in verse 39.

In verse 40, Jesus gently rebuked the disciples for their lack of faith in Him. He was with them in the very same boat, in their very same circumstances. Surely they didn't really doubt His care for them or His ability to deal with those circumstances?

Here is a key message in this section. The One who is the perfect Servant is also the One who has supreme power, unlike an ordinary servant. As the Son of God, He is creator of all things (Colossians 1:16) and everything must obey the word of His power. Not only does He have power over the forces in creation as seen in this last section of Mark 4, but if we were to read chapter 5 we would see in His further miracles that He has power over demons, over disease and over death, whether in man, woman or child.

The disciples ask in the last verse of our chapter:

> "What manner of man is this, that even the wind and the sea obey him?"

The wonder of this One whom they followed was being revealed progressively to them.

And what for me? Do I seek to model myself and my service for God on the perfect Servant of Mark's Gospel? Do I faithfully sow the word of God recognising that God alone can give the increase? Do I show the light of my new life to the world around? Can I answer from my heart the disciples' question, "What manner of man is this?"

May each of us who has heard and received the word of God seek to be real servants of the One who is both the perfect Servant and the mighty Son of God.

John 18

Series: Studies in John's Gospel

Broadcast date: 9th March 2008

The last four chapters of the Gospel cover the arrest, trial, crucifixion and resurrection of Jesus as well as His final appearances to His disciples.

I would like to start with a reminder that each of the four Gospels portrays a particular aspect of the Lord Jesus. In Matthew He is presented as *King*, in Mark as the *Servant* and in Luke as the *Son of Man*. Those three Gospels are sometimes referred to as the synoptic Gospels meaning that they present Jesus in a broadly similar way, if with a different emphasis in each. John's Gospel is different. Jesus is presented as the *Son of God*. Right from the very first verse, His divine origin is stated and the book is full of statements about His Person, many of which are not repeated in the other three Gospels. Aspects of that are seen in these last four chapters.

In chapters 13 to 17, Jesus spends much time with those who are described as "His own", telling them of great things which could only be told to those who belong to

Him. Many of the words are spoken on the way to the Garden of Gethsemane and it is the arrival at the Garden with which chapter 18, our subject, commences.

I would like to structure our consideration around the four individuals with whom Jesus had most to do in chapter 18. There were other individuals and there were groups of people as well, but most attention is drawn to:

- Judas the friend and betrayer;
- Caiaphas the priest;
- Peter the disciple and denier;
- Pilate the governor.

At the same time, I want to try to draw attention to some of the ways in which John's theme of Jesus as the Son of God is brought out in this chapter. Under each of our four headings we will look at one or more verses.

JUDAS THE FRIEND AND BETRAYER

So, to our first heading, which covers verses 1-12. Let's read verses 1-6:

> "When Jesus had spoken these words, he went forth with his disciples over the brook Cedron, where was a garden, into the which he entered, and his disciples. And Judas also, which betrayed him, knew the place: for Jesus ofttimes resorted thither with his disciples. Judas then, having received a band of men and officers from the chief priests and Pharisees, cometh thither with lanterns and torches and weapons. Jesus therefore, knowing all things that should come upon him, went forth, and said unto them, Whom seek ye? They answered him, Jesus of Nazareth. Jesus saith unto them, I am he. And Judas also, which betrayed him, stood with them. As soon then as

he had said unto them, I am he, they went backward, and fell to the ground."

John does not record the Lord's agony in prayer in the Garden of Gethsemane but concentrates on the betrayal and arrest of Jesus. Judas is mentioned three times in these first 12 verses and in two of the instances it is added "which betrayed him". Here was a man who had journeyed with Jesus for three years, had seen for himself the miracles which Jesus had performed, had heard for himself the words which Jesus said and had witnessed for himself the love and grace which Jesus showed to those in need. And yet here Judas is, in cowardly fashion at night, leading a group of armed men to betray that same Jesus!

I feel that I must draw attention to the danger of someone mixing closely with Christians, hearing and perhaps knowing the words of the Bible, even acting like a Christian, and yet like Judas, not having that personal relationship with Jesus which is the only thing which makes a real Christian. Dear reader, I hope that you are not like Judas, pretending and looking fine on the surface, but in reality not having trusted in Jesus as Saviour and Lord in a real way. What a warning Judas is!

Earlier, I referred to Judas as friend as well as betrayer. I have in mind the prophecy of Psalm 41:9 which reads:

> "Yea, mine own familiar friend, in whom I trusted, which did eat of my bread, hath lifted up his heel against me."

We sometimes may forget what sadness it brought to Jesus to have this friend betray Him, someone who seemed close to Him and yet in the end sided with His enemies.

Now, to mention a few things in John 18:1-12 which continue the emphasis in this Gospel of Jesus as the Son of God. Firstly, in verse 4 it says that

"Jesus therefore, knowing all things that should come upon him, went forth".

As Son of God, there was nothing of the horrifying events to come which Jesus did not know, yet still Jesus positively "went forth" to those who would arrest Him.

Then, in response to the arrestors' statement that the One whom they sought was Jesus of Nazareth, Jesus said, "I am." In the Authorised Version the words are recorded in verse 5 as "I am he" but that third word is not in the original and the statement should simply but profoundly be: "I am." Jesus had previously used this statement of Himself in John 8:58 when He said:

"Before Abraham was, I am",

thereby linking Himself with God, who told Moses to take the message into Egypt that

"I AM hath sent me" (Exodus 3:14).

Jesus was stating to these men in the Garden that He was and is the eternal Son of God, equal with God. The impact of this statement on these men was dramatic – "they went backward, and fell to the ground" (verse 6).

Jesus, as Son of God, knew that He must go forward to the cross to finish the work which His Father had given Him to do (17:4). Peter did not have this divine perception and so tried to protect Jesus by using his sword to cut off the ear of Malchus, one of the high priest's servants, as recorded in verses 10-11 of our chapter. Naturally speaking, this seemed an applaudable action by Peter, but Jesus would not have anyone or anything interfere with His determination to go forward to Calvary.

The suggestion from verses 3 & 12, is that the company which came to arrest Jesus was of a reasonable size. Whatever their size and weaponry, we see from the power of the Son of God that, while they thought that they arrested and overcame Jesus, in fact they could have done nothing if He had not allowed them to do so!

CAIAPHAS THE PRIEST

We come now to the second main individual in this chapter, Caiaphas the priest. The account of Caiaphas is covered in verses 13-14 & 19-24. We'll read verses 14 & 19-21:

> "Now Caiaphas was he, which gave counsel to the Jews, that it was expedient that one man should die for the people. ... The high priest then asked Jesus of his disciples, and of his doctrine. Jesus answered him, I spake openly to the world; I ever taught in the synagogue, and in the temple, whither the Jews always resort; and in secret have I said nothing. Why askest thou me? ask them which heard me, what I have said unto them: behold, they know what I said."

It seems that when the Romans conquered a particular territory they would tolerate the continuance of local religions as long as these did not pose a threat to the Roman rule. The Romans preferred to have in place as religious leader a local person of their choice and this is how Caiaphas achieved office as high priest. There was no Old Testament basis for this appointment. In effect he was a political choice for a religious position.

From being arrested and bound in Gethesemane, Jesus is taken via Annas to his son in law, Caiaphas. Caiaphas questions Jesus about His disciples and His doctrine. Jesus does not say anything about His disciples, continuing to protect them. Of His doctrine, Jesus told Caiaphas that He had always spoken openly, including in the Jewish synagogue and temple, to the many who had heard Him. Caiaphas should enquire of them to determine what Jesus had said of His doctrine and whether there was anything of evil in it.

In John 11:47-53, following Jesus raising Lazarus from the dead, the chief priests and Pharisees met to discuss their concern that more and more people would follow Jesus because of His many miracles. This would cause concern to the Romans who could then take action to remove the religion and identity of the Jews. At that meeting, Caiaphas said that it would be better for the Jews if one person, Jesus, were killed rather than the whole Jewish people be put at risk. Little did Caiaphas realise that he was uttering words which were in God's purpose for blessing for all nations through the death of Jesus.

Taking those verses in John 11 with these in chapter 18, it seems clear that Caiaphas had decided in advance that Jesus needed to die. The Romans did not allow the Jews to implement the death sentence; and to get rid of Jesus the Jews therefore needed Pilate to pronounce that sentence. In this meeting with Jesus recorded in chapter 18, Caiaphas was looking for any pretext which would allow him to present to the Roman Governor a case for Jesus being put to death. We know from reading the other Gospels that the religious leaders of the Jews tried hard to find witnesses, true or false, who would be willing to allege that Jesus had made public statements which were evil. Jesus, Son of God, could see right into the mind of Caiaphas and knew exactly what that scheming man was trying to achieve.

I believe that Caiaphas is a warning to us that to be a Christian leader, even by political appointment, does not of itself mean that that leader is a born again Christian. Essentially, Caiaphas was no better than Judas, despite his title of high priest and his religious trappings. For every person of whatever religious standing, the Bible teaches that it is essential to have a personal relationship with Jesus, based on His death on the cross for the sins of everyone, including religious leaders.

PETER THE DISCIPLE AND DENIER

Now we turn to the third individual in this chapter, and the verses we need to look at are 15-18 & 25-27. Verses 15-16 tell us that the disciples, Peter and John, followed Jesus after His arrest but at a distance. John was able to gain access for himself and Peter to the high priest's residence. We pick up the reading from verse 17:

"Then saith the damsel that kept the door unto Peter, Art not thou also one of this man's disciples? He saith, I am not. And the servants and officers stood there, who had made a fire of coals; for it was cold: and they warmed themselves: and Peter stood with them, and warmed himself."

And now to verse 25:

"And Simon Peter stood and warmed himself. They said therefore unto him, Art not thou also one of his disciples? He denied it, and said, I am not. One of the servants of the high priest, being his kinsman whose ear Peter cut off, saith, Did not

I see thee in the garden with him? Peter then
denied again: and immediately the cock crew."

These verses tell us of the sad event of Peter three times
denying Jesus. In each of the other three Gospels there
is a record of Jesus telling Peter that shortly he would
deny the Lord, for example in Matthew 26:34. As Son of
God, Jesus knew everything and it is no surprise then
that we read in these verses of the fulfilment of the
Lord's prediction.

There are lessons in this for us. At a time of difficulty in
following the Lord, Peter was in the wrong place with
the wrong people. Spiritually speaking, he was trying to
get help from people who couldn't help him, because
they were not followers of Jesus and at a fire which may
have been physically warm but which did nothing to
warm him spiritually. And so he got into deep water
when questioned by non-believers about his relationship with Jesus. He should have been with the other
disciples.

Can you relate to any of this? I can. Sometimes in my
Christian life when all has not been well, instead of getting back to the Word of God, to prayer and to other
believers, I haven't and a poor situation has got worse.

There is another, perhaps less obvious, lesson. John was
in broadly the same situation as Peter. In fact it was John
who gained access for Peter to the high priest's residence. It seems that John could withstand the pressures
of that place whereas Peter couldn't. As Christians we
differ in what can cause us to fail. Satan is well aware of
the weaknesses of each of us and he may tempt me with
things which differ from those with which he tempts
you. Let us try to be careful, particularly with Christians
who may be under pressure or who have not belonged

to the Lord for very long, not to put them into situations which could cause them to stumble.

I have to say that I can relate to Peter. He acted first, then thought about it. He was impulsive. He took a long time to realise that his own strength wasn't good enough and that he had to see things spiritually and not just naturally. But, to use an expression, his heart was in the right place. Peter was a disciple and the word disciple means learner. Peter did learn and when we come to the Acts of the Apostles we see what a tremendous servant of God Peter becomes, after his failings recorded in the Gospels and his interview with the Lord recorded in John 21. There three times Jesus asks Peter, "Do you love me", just as three times in our chapter Peter denied the Lord. The Son of God sees the potential in those who belong to Him and that potential can be realised if our relationship with Him is right.

PILATE THE GOVERNOR

Lastly, we come to Pilate the governor, from verse 28 to the end of the chapter. I can't think of anyone in the Bible worse than Pilate for trying to please everybody, for realising the reality but refusing to face up to it, for hiding behind clever words, for trying to get rid of personal responsibility by attempting to pass it on to somebody else. I certainly wouldn't want my destiny to be in the hands of someone like Pilate! But he was an ideal man for the Jews to use to progress this travesty of a trial of Jesus. In the ways of God's wonderful plan of salvation, Jesus had to die, innocent though He was.

Let's read verse 28:

> "Then led they Jesus from Caiaphas unto the hall of judgment: and it was early; and they themselves

went not into the judgment hall, lest they should be defiled; but that they might eat the passover."

This verse underlines the sheer hypocrisy of the religious leaders of the day. They were concerned to keep the formal rituals to stay clean, but were quite happy to resort to lies and deceit to get rid of Jesus. Everyone who calls himself a Christian should be careful to ensure that he is a real believer in Jesus and not hide behind a lot of procedures which are mere ritual.

The thrust of Pilate's initial questioning of Jesus in verses 33-36 was to ascertain whether Jesus was looking to establish Himself as a King of the Jewish nation and therefore be a rival to Cæsar.

Verse 36 contains the answer of Jesus to this accusation:

"My kingdom is not of this world: if my kingdom were of this world, then would my servants fight, that I should not be delivered to the Jews: but now is my kingdom not from hence."

Jesus had already told His listeners some time earlier:

"Ye are from beneath; I am from above: ye are of this world; I am not of this world" (John 8:23).

Jesus, the Son of God, was from heaven and therefore His kingdom was heavenly and was spiritual in nature. It would not be established by man's weapons of war but is established by God's decree and the Bible teaches that God will evidence this to the world in a future day when Jesus will be seen as King of kings, and Lord of lords (Revelation 19:16). So, once again John's emphasis on the divine nature of Jesus is seen in our chapter.

The message of a section of the Bible can sometimes be determined by noting the frequency of occurrence of a word or a phrase. For example, a typical phrase in John's

Gospel is "I am", stating the divine attributes of the Son of God. If you have a Bible concordance, look up the word 'truth' and you will see that, while it scarcely appears in the first three Gospels, it occurs many times in John's Gospel. Nothing in the Bible is there by coincidence and I suggest that the Holy Spirit is here drawing attention to the fact that the Son of God is the very embodiment of truth. Perhaps the best known example in John is 14:6 where Jesus says:

"I am the way, the truth, and the life: ..."

In verses 37-38 of our chapter this matter of truth is raised. There Jesus said that He came

"into the world, that I should bear witness unto the truth."

Pilate typically avoided the issue by asking the philosophical question "What is truth?" and then walking away from the One who was truth personified.

Pilate walked away from Jesus and went outside to the Jews with his verdict: "I find in him no fault at all." This seems a final judgement from the governor; however it was followed by a "but" when, in the final two verses of our chapter, Pilate tried to pass the buck by leaving the final choice to the people as to whether Jesus should be released. Their choice was between Jesus and Barabbas. Instead of the Son of God the people chose Barabbas. The chapter closes with the salutary comment on that choice: "Now Barabbas was a robber."

As with the other individuals we have considered in this chapter, Pilate is a warning to us. He would not stand up for what he knew to be right because it could cause him difficulties. He hid behind clever questions, such as "What is truth?" He tried to pass on the ultimate responsibility for the death of an innocent Jesus to others. Dear readers, let us be absolutely clear that the Bible teaches that each of us personally will have to answer to God as to what we think of Jesus. There will be no wriggling out of it by using clever words or walking away or blaming others!

While these four individuals all disappointed to a greater or lesser extent, I want to end by pointing to the central Person in this chapter, Jesus, the Son of God. He never disappointed. He lived a perfect life. He was faithful to God in being determined to go on to Calvary. And yet, as we see in chapter 19, Jesus is

"the Son of God, who loved me, and gave himself for me" (Galatians 2:20).

Godliness in an ungodly age – Daniel 5

SERIES: 21ST CENTURY CHALLENGES FROM DANIEL

BROADCAST DATE: 18TH MAY 2008

The first five chapters of Daniel can be given the headings:

Daniel 1	Faithfulness to God;
Daniel 2	God's plan of the ages;
Daniel 3	God or idolatry;
Daniel 4	Lowliness or self-assertiveness;
Daniel 5	Godliness in an ungodly age.

In about 600 BC, the mightiest empire in the world was Babylon, which was roughly where Iraq is now. The leader of the empire of Babylon was King Nebuchadnezzar. The king twice attacked Jerusalem, taking away various treasures and holy vessels from the temple there and also a substantial number of captives. Among these captives was Daniel, who was a prince in his own country. The holy vessels from the temple in Jerusalem were put into the temples of the false gods of Babylon and the lives of the Jewish captives were greatly changed as pressure was put on them to conform to the attitudes and false religions of the land in which they were held prisoner. They were in a country to which they did not belong and they were being pressurised to live as those in that country did rather than be true to the God of Israel.

This is the background to Daniel 5, where the events recorded probably took place round about 550 BC. The story of the chapter has dramatic, miraculous and sad elements. It has long been one of my favourite Bible stories and the excitement of it can be readily conveyed to children and young people. However, as with all Bible stories, it has messages for us today. Let us be clear that this story is not a fable and it is not just for children. The events really did happen and God today wants to speak through those events to all of us.

THE EVENTS IN DANIEL 5

Let me first of all summarise the events of the chapter and then see what we can learn from these about our subject, 'Godliness in an ungodly age'. I want to start with Daniel 5:1-6:

> "Belshazzar the king made a great feast to a thousand of his lords, and drank wine before the thousand. Belshazzar, whiles he tasted the wine, commanded to bring the golden and silver vessels which his father Nebuchadnezzar had taken out of the temple which was in Jerusalem; that the king, and his princes, his wives, and his concubines, might drink therein. Then they brought the golden vessels that were taken out of the temple of the house of God which was at Jerusalem; and the king, and his princes, his wives, and his concubines, drank in them. They drank wine, and praised the gods of gold, and of silver, of brass, of

iron, of wood, and of stone. In the same hour came forth fingers of a man's hand, and wrote over against the candlestick upon the plaister of the wall of the king's palace: and the king saw the part of the hand that wrote. Then the king's countenance was changed, and his thoughts troubled him, so that the joints of his loins were loosed, and his knees smote one against another."

The chapter goes on to tell that the king couldn't understand the words written on the wall by the fingers of the hand. He called in his wise men to help in the interpretation of the words, offering a reward to the successful interpreter. None of these wise men could help. The king was not best pleased and in fact was quite alarmed. Seeing this, the queen recommended Daniel, using the following words recorded in verses 11-12:

"There is a man in thy kingdom, in whom is the spirit of the holy gods; and in the days of thy father light and understanding and wisdom, like the wisdom of the gods, was found in him; whom the king Nebuchadnezzar thy father, the king, I say, thy father, made master of the magicians, astrologers, Chaldeans, and soothsayers; forasmuch as an excellent spirit, and knowledge, and understanding, interpreting of dreams, and shewing of hard sentences, and dissolving of doubts, were found in the same Daniel, whom the king named Belteshazzar: now let Daniel be called, and he will shew the interpretation."

Daniel was brought to the king and first of all said that he did not want the king's reward. Then, as recorded in verses 18-21, Daniel summarised God's dealings with King Nebuchadnezzar, Belshazzar's grandfather; incidentally, the Old Testament uses the word *father*, as it does in this chapter, in the sense of 'forefather'. That summary of God's dealings with Nebuchadnezzar is important and we will return to it later.

Daniel then bravely goes on directly to confront Belshazzar as to his own pride and disregard for the things of God in the words of verses 22-23:

> "And thou his son, O Belshazzar, hast not humbled thine heart, though thou knewest all this; but hast lifted up thyself against the Lord of heaven; and they have brought the vessels of his house before thee, and thou, and thy lords, thy wives, and thy concubines, have drunk wine in them; and thou hast praised the gods of silver, and gold, of brass, iron, wood, and stone, which see not, nor hear, nor know: and the God in whose hand thy breath is, and whose are all thy ways, hast thou not glorified".

Daniel finally pronounces the words written on the wall by the fingers of the hand together with the meanings of those words. The words were Mene, Mene, Tekel, Upharsin. The meanings were:

- Mene – "God hath numbered thy kingdom, and finished it";
- Tekel – "Thou art weighed in the balances, and art found wanting";
- Peres, which is the singular form of Upharsin – "Thy kingdom is divided, and given to the Medes and Persians."

Solemnly, the chapter ends with the record that that very night King Belshazzar was killed. That was the end of the dominance of the empire of Babylon. The dominance was then taken over by the empire of the Medes and Persians.

WHAT IS GODLINESS?

As I said earlier, our subject is 'Godliness in an ungodly age.' I would like to spend a short time considering what *godliness* is. In Paul's letters in the New Testament, he only uses the word 'godliness' when writing to two individuals, Timothy and Titus, and particularly in his first letter to Timothy. I take it from this that *godliness is an individual matter.* *Doctrine* is another word used fairly frequently in 1 Timothy. Doctrine means 'teaching', that is, teaching the substance of something. Paul, the apostle, had sent Timothy to Ephesus to ensure that the church there was being reminded of good and sound doctrine. Paul said to Timothy (1 Timothy 3:16):

"… great is the mystery of godliness"

and then goes on in the remainder of that verse to write about Christ being

"… manifest in the flesh, justified in the Spirit, seen of angels, preached unto the Gentiles, believed on in the world, received up into glory."

From all of this, it seems to me that an individual's godliness stems from an inward appreciation of everything to do with Christ, which then demonstrates itself by a life which is pleasing to Christ and which is consistent with the doctrine of Scripture.

Mr W. E. Vine in his *Complete Expository Dictionary of Old and New Testament Words* explains godliness as "piety which, characterised by a Godward attitude, does that which is well-pleasing to Him." It is a practical word, an outward demonstration of what a Christian inwardly is enjoying of Christ.

AN UNGODLY SOCIETY

With that brief consideration of godliness, we return to Daniel 5 and our subject 'Godliness in an ungodly age.' If ungodliness is the opposite of godliness, there can be little doubt that Babylon, where Daniel was held captive, was an ungodly country. Let's just note five examples from Daniel 5 to illustrate the ungodliness of that society.

1.   Verses 1-3 tell of the holy vessels from the temple in Jerusalem being used as ordinary drinking vessels at the king's feast. These holy vessels of Old Testament times had been made for God's holy purposes as instructed by God. We note that the society in which Daniel lived took no account, no notice, of what God instructed.

2.   Verse 4 tells us that as they drank wine at the feast from the holy vessels, they "praised the gods of gold, and of silver, of brass, of iron, of wood, and of stone." With no consideration of the only true God, the God of heaven, they praised and gave idol status to material things.

3.   When faced with a problem in not being able to interpret the writing on the wall, they did not immediately seek God's help, but turned to those representing the wisdom of the world, the astrologers, the Chaldeans, the soothsayers – the wise men of Babylon (verse 7). Divine wisdom was way down on their scale of importance and it was only in extremity of circumstances that the queen brought to the attention of the king, Daniel, the servant of "the most high God", the phrase used in verse 18.

4.   They ignored the lessons which God had taught King Nebuchadnezzar, another king of Babylon who was full of pride and self-importance, who considered himself to be above everyone, including the most high God. Verses 18-21 of our chapter describe Nebuchadnezzar's view of himself and then the dramatic actions God took to bring Nebuchadnezzar down. Daniel told Belshazzar that, despite knowing all this, he had not humbled his own heart (verse 22).

5.   Belshazzar thought that anything and everything could be bought with the reward of enhanced status. He offered this to the wise men of Babylon (verse 7) and to Daniel (verse 16), if any could interpret the writing on the wall. In that society, status before men mattered much more than a person's standing before God.

Now, those examples have been taken from this chapter which describes a society more than 2,500 years ago. Yet what strikes me is that we could be describing society today!

1.   The first example I took from Daniel 5:1-3 tells us that the people then, including those in authority, *took no notice of what God instructed.* God's instructions to us today are set out in His word, the Bible. Is the Bible generally followed in our world today? I think not. For example, God's instructions as to the Lord's Day, marriage, obeying parents and Jesus Christ being the only way to God are widely ignored. Even those who say that they accept the Bible sometimes pick and choose which parts they will accept, and this at times by those who purport to be Christian leaders. In the eyes of some, science is all that matters and the

WHAT A GOD WE CHRISTIANS HAVE!

essential place of faith as taught in the Bible is out of date, whereas God says about His word that it "liveth and abideth for ever" (1 Peter 1:23). In other words, the Bible is always relevant and applicable, whatever the world thinks today.

2. The second example, from Daniel 5:4, showed that the people and the leaders of Babylon *made idols of material things*, giving no consideration to the only true God. And what of today? My clear impression is of a world where material wealth is a god for many. The people in today's headlines tend to be those with wealth. Rich people in the entertainment and business fields are sometimes turned into idols. The dream of many is to win the lottery. The Bible says of those who became Christians in the city of Thessalonica that they "turned to God from idols to serve the living and true God; and to wait for his Son from heaven" (1 Thessalonians 1:9-10).

3. Example three was taken from Daniel 5:7 where, when faced with a problem, the leader in Babylon *did not first turn to God* but turned to those representing the wisdom of the world. Those people couldn't help. The Bible says that worldly wisdom "descendeth not from above, but is earthly, sensual (or natural)," even "devilish" (James 3:15). It seems that many will not acknowledge that, even with the best intentions and endeavours, man's wisdom just can't resolve many problems, particularly those which stem from sin. Only the God of heaven is capable of dealing with these things.

4. In example four, from Daniel 5:18-22, we noted that Belshazzar and his people ignored the lessons which God had taught Nebuchadnezzar in the

past. In Britain, we have a great Christian heritage and God has blessed this country in many ways. Some people who lived through World War 2 have told me that churches then were packed as people sought God's help in a time of extreme circumstances. Now the lessons of our past and the lessons from the Bible are being ignored. In many schools lessons from the Bible are watered down, if allowed at all. Complacently and dangerously, just like Belshazzar, we *ignore what God has shown us.*

5. Finally, the fifth example taken from Daniel 5:7 & 16 showed that in Babylon *status before men mattered more than standing before God.* Today also, pride sometimes drives people to want to equal or better the wealth, possessions and power of others – the "keeping up with the Jones's" syndrome. God says that the status of everyone in His sight is that "all have sinned, and come short of the glory of God" (Romans 3:23). I can't have God's eternal salvation until I recognise that I am a worthless sinner and desperately need that salvation.

I suggest, therefore, that there are many similarities between Babylon and the world today. I suggest that both were or are godless societies. Let us read what the Bible says in 2 Timothy 3:1-5 and see whether we can identify the world today from what God says:

"This know also, that in the last days perilous times shall come. For men shall be lovers of their own selves, covetous, boasters, proud, blasphemers, disobedient to parents, unthankful, unholy, without natural affection, trucebreakers, false accusers, incontinent, fierce, despisers of those that are good, traitors, heady, highminded, lovers of pleasures more than lovers of God; having a form of godliness, but denying the power thereof".

Our subject is 'Godliness in an ungodly age.' The challenge to Daniel was to demonstrate godliness when around him society demonstrated that it was ungodly. That is also the challenge to me in an ungodly world today. Let's see if we can gain some help from Daniel's example.

DANIEL'S GODLY EXAMPLE

It is clear from the earlier chapters of this book that *Daniel lived close to God*. In his heart he was determined to live for God (1:8). He acknowledged God's goodness and praised Him (2:19-23). And we can see from chapter 6 that Daniel was a man of prayer. Daniel had a close inward personal relationship with God and therefore outwardly was able to display godliness in his life, whatever the circumstances around him. In the same way, if I want to live a godly life in this ungodly age, I have to spend time regularly in communion with Christ, learning and appreciating more about Him and His ways. From that deep, personal relationship will flow a display of godliness in my life.

Then, I notice that *Daniel's testimony for God was consistent*. He had taken a stand for God, he understood the nature of God and he did not waver from consistently demonstrating the qualities appropriate to a follower of God. He was not up and down depending on how he felt. As he had been in Nebuchadnezzar's day, so he was in the time of Belshazzar, so that the queen could point to Daniel's longstanding godly qualities (Daniel 5:10-12). Daniel's manner of life matched his words. I wonder if this is true of me? Is my manner of life always consistent in a display of godliness, where actions are in line with my stated belief in the Bible and what it says?

I also notice that *Daniel was separate from the wise men of the kingdom of Babylon.* They were given the first opportunity to interpret the words on the wall. Daniel was called in on his own later. The ways and beliefs of those worldly wise men would not have helped Daniel live for God. Similarly, there is a challenge for me as a Christian to be separate from those things in the world today which would adversely affect my wish to live a godly life. When I was younger, I was often told that I should be "in the world and not of it". Daniel was like that.

Daniel also wasn't interested in the reward which Belshazzar offered for an interpretation of the words. Worldly wealth and status didn't interest Daniel, though he had been brought up as a prince in Jerusalem. He declined the king's reward (verse 17). Here is a challenge for me today! If my heart is set on achieving wealth and status in this world, this must cause a conflict with living for God. Daniel was single minded about this.

Daniel had also taken note of God's dealings in the past and, unlike Belshazzar, hadn't ignored the lessons to be taken from these. I wonder whether I not only know my Bible and the record in it of what God expects, but also whether I then allow that knowledge to affect the way in which I live. The standards of the world change and usually, in my experience, not for the better. God's standards never change and those who would live godly lives need to follow those standards, whatever the changes that occur in the world around.

Lastly, I note *Daniel's bravery in speaking out for God.* He was very straight in speaking to Belshazzar in the way that he did as recorded in verses 22-23. He literally risked his life with that powerful king. The challenge to me is to stand up and speak up clearly for God in an ungodly world.

Nowhere in the book of Daniel does it suggest that displaying godliness is easy. Standing up for God is often displayed in the Bible as a battle. Those who emerge victorious are those who stay close to Christ.

While it is outside the scope of our subject, I feel that I can't finish without drawing attention to the solemn end to this chapter. Belshazzar had ignored and disobeyed God. God weighed Belshazzar in the balances and found him wanting. God judged Belshazzar and verse 30 records that that very night Belshazzar was slain. Galatians 6:7 states that:

> "... God is not mocked: for whatsoever a man soweth, that shall he also reap."

Belshazzar found that to be true when it was too late. I do hope that no reader of this message today ignores the truth of these things.

May each of us know what it is to be right with God through our Lord Jesus Christ. In that way, may we know the power to live for Him in this ungodly world.

Pentecost – Acts 2

SERIES: KEY EVENTS IN THE ACTS

BROADCAST DATE: 27TH JULY 2008

At school, I enjoyed learning about history. Not so much in learning about a string of dates and names, but gradually growing to appreciate that particular events had a fundamental impact on the development of nations and of commerce. Some of the unhappy situations which exist in the world today can be traced back to past events, some of them occurring many centuries ago.

If we were to select "Key events in the Acts" – referring of course to the Acts of the Apostles, the fifth book in the New Testament – there are four events we might choose:

Acts 2	Pentecost;
Acts 9	the conversion of Paul;
Acts 10	the Gospel first preached to Gentiles;
Acts 16	the first Christian conversions in Europe.

It is no exaggeration to call each of these a key event in Christian history, because each has far-reaching and lasting effects, the results of which are seen today, almost 2,000 years after the events took place. There is no suggestion that these are the only key events recorded in the 28 chapters of the Acts, merely that these four are among the most notable.

MOMENTOUS TIMES

We must spend a little time reminding ourselves of how momentous those times in the Acts were when considering God's dealings with mankind as recorded in the Bible. The period of time when God judged mankind on their ability to meet the requirements of the law had ended. That period of time included much of the Old Testament and covered many centuries. Jesus Christ, God's Son, had been born as a man, had lived, had died at Calvary, had risen from the dead and had ascended back to heaven; see the Gospels of Matthew, Mark, Luke and John. From this point, God calls all men everywhere to repent – not to earn salvation, but to receive the free gift of eternal life through faith in Jesus. From here on, the Gospel of the grace of God will be preached, starting the period of time when God deals with mankind on the principle of God's grace, not of His law. This period of time, still going on today, is sometimes referred to as *the day of salvation* and will last until Jesus returns as set out in 1 Thessalonians 4:15-17, fulfilling the words of Jesus Himself when He said, in John 14:3:

"I will come again, and receive you unto myself…".

Those were thrilling if challenging times for the followers of Jesus. The first church was established (Acts 2:42-47). There was great blessing as many became Christians – see Acts 2:41 and 4:4, for example. The Gospel was forcefully preached to all people of whatever category, for example by Peter to the Jewish religious leaders when he said (Acts 4:12):

"Neither is there salvation in any other: for there is none other name under heaven given among men, whereby we must be saved."

The believers in Jesus displayed Christ in their lives to such effect that, in Antioch, they gained the nickname of "Christians" (Acts 11:26), that is Christ-like ones, and in Thessalonica the apostles and others, as recorded in Acts 17:6, were referred to as

"These that have turned the world upside down…".

God displayed His power through many miracles at this time, for example the healing of the lame man in Acts 3.

TRANSITIONAL TIMES

It is important to realise that for most of the period of time covered by the Acts, the New Testament Scriptures had not been written. God's truth for His people was being taught by the apostles – those specially sent forth by God – divinely inspired to teach foundation truth and those who were unique to that period of time. When Paul on his missionary journeys preached the Gospel and there were those who believed in Christ, he usually then spent time with those converts to teach them the basic truths of the faith and sometimes subsequently sent others, for example Timothy and Titus, to ensure that that teaching was understood and being followed. He sometimes later wrote to those new churches to help build them up in their faith, and some of those letters (or *epistles*) now form part of the New Testament.

So, those times in the Acts were transitional times when great and new truths were being revealed and explained. Remember also that most of the first Christians were Jews and the first Christian church was formed in Jerusalem, the very centre of the Jewish religion. The Jews had been God's *earthly* people for centuries and were used to considering themselves as the only ones favoured in God's sight. It must have been hugely difficult for them even to realise, let alone accept, that in this new day of salvation no longer were the Jews to be specially favoured before God, but that every individual in the world, through repentance and faith in Christ, could become part of God's *heavenly* people. Little wonder that the Jews showed as much hostility to Christians in the Acts as they had to Christ at Calvary. And most of the hostility was led by the Jewish religious leaders.

I have spent a fair amount of time emphasising the fundamental differences being brought in at that time. This is crucial background to our topic.

OLD TESTAMENT BACKGROUND

Our subject here is *Pentecost* and I would like to start by going back into the Old Testament, to Leviticus 23. In that chapter, God is instructing the Children of Israel, the Jews, to introduce 7 feasts to celebrate and give thanks to God for particular aspects of His dealings with them. As with much of Old Testament teaching, each of these feasts points forward to an aspect of New Testament teaching. The first three feasts are of the *passover, unleavened bread* and *firstfruits*, that third feast of firstfruits pointing forward to Christ's resurrection. There then comes the fourth feast, the feast of *wave loaves,* to take place 50 days after the previous feast. The word *Pentecost* means 'fiftieth' and just as feasts three and four were to be separated by 50 days, so Pentecost in the Acts took place 50 days after Christ's resurrection from the dead. I don't know about you, but I never cease to be impressed with how the whole Bible fits together so perfectly and how God's plans for the future are so accurately pictured in events that took place in Old Testament times. Pentecost in the book of Acts was not an event which occurred at a haphazard time. It was something which God had planned and it occurred exactly in accordance with His timing!

A key New Testament event

The event of Pentecost is described in Acts 2:1-12 and we must read most of the exact words, only for the sake of time missing out part of verses 9-11 which set out the various languages in which those believers suddenly were empowered to speak:

> "And when the day of Pentecost was fully come, they were all with one accord in one place. And suddenly there came a sound from heaven as of a rushing mighty wind, and it filled all the house where they were sitting. And there appeared unto them cloven tongues like as of fire, and it sat upon each of them. And they were all filled with the Holy Ghost, and began to speak with other tongues, as the Spirit gave them utterance. And there were dwelling at Jerusalem Jews, devout men, out of every nation under heaven. Now when this was noised abroad, the multitude came together, and were confounded, because that every man heard them speak in his own language. And they were all amazed and marvelled, saying one to another, Behold, are not all these which speak Galilaeans? And how hear we every man in our own tongue, wherein we were born? ... we do

hear them speak in our tongues the wonderful works of God. And they were all amazed, and were in doubt, saying one to another, What meaneth this?"

As recorded in verse 1, all the believers were gathered together on the day of Pentecost. The word "all" would refer to the 120 mentioned in Acts 1:15 and not just to the apostles. They were gathered together in Jerusalem in obedience and expectation because, before Jesus ascended back to heaven, He instructed, in Luke 24:49:

"And, behold, I send the promise of my Father upon you: but tarry ye in the city of Jerusalem, until ye be endued with power from on high."

Earlier (John 14:16-17), Jesus had told His disciples:

"And I will pray the Father, and he shall give you another Comforter, that he may abide with you for ever; even the Spirit of truth; whom the world cannot receive, because it seeth him not, neither knoweth him: but ye know him; for he dwelleth with you, and shall be in you."

Pentecost is the time when that promise was fulfilled. When Jesus used the phrase "another Comforter", I understand that the word *another* means 'one of the same kind'. In other words, though Jesus had departed to heaven, another Person equally as great as Jesus would descend and abide – remain, stay – with them for ever. This Person is the Holy Spirit, referred to as the Comforter, or One called alongside to help.

In the verses we have read from Acts 2, the Holy Spirit descended with sounds and signs of power, a rushing mighty wind and tongues like as of fire. The believers were enabled to speak languages which they had never learned, maybe never even heard. The One who descended was indeed a Person of power, who would now indwell all believers, enabling them to live for God.

This was a *permanent* indwelling. When David of the Old Testament realised that he had sinned so grievously in his actions to obtain Bathsheba as his wife, Psalm 51 records his prayer of repentance, including in verse 11 the words "take not thy holy spirit from me." In Old Testament times the Holy Spirit came on followers of God, but not permanently. From Pentecost onwards, the Spirit permanently dwells in Christians. It would be completely inappropriate for a Christian to use David's prayer today. Pentecost was indeed a key event!

The power of the event was demonstrated to non-believers by the God-given ability of these ordinary believers, not just to speak in a different dialect, but to speak a range of foreign languages as though they were native to each language. This was heard not just by a few but by a multitude of people. God had caused confusion of languages because of man's arrogance displayed at the Tower of Babel in Genesis 11; now God the Holy Spirit further displays His control over languages at this time. Verse 7 of our chapter says that the people "were all amazed and marvelled".

Pentecost is significant from another aspect. In Acts 1:5, it is recorded that Jesus had said to His disciples:

> "ye shall be baptised with the Holy Ghost not many days hence."

We need to be clear that the Bible phrase 'the baptism of the Holy Spirit' refers to Pentecost and to nothing else. In 1 Corinthians 12:13 the Bible says:

> "For by one Spirit are we all baptised into one body…"

125

Nobody becomes part of the body of Christ until they receive the Holy Spirit on conversion. These Scriptures would combine to teach us that the church began at Pentecost and that, on conversion, when each Christian receives the Holy Spirit, a believer becomes part of the body of Christ, the church. When I am converted, it is not exactly that I am baptised with the Holy Spirit. As mentioned, that baptism of the Spirit took place once, at Pentecost. Rather, I think the idea is that on conversion I come into the good of the baptism of the Spirit, which has already taken place.

The wording of Acts 2:2-3 is interesting. In verse 2, it says that the sound from heaven "filled all the house". All the believers then living were present in that house and they all were immersed in that sound, just like being immersed in water at baptism. It wasn't an experience involving those outside the house; they were not believers. So this baptism of the Spirit formed the church. Then in verse 3 it says that the "cloven tongues like as of fire ... sat upon each of them". This would emphasise the aspect of the work of the Spirit in individual believers, empowering each for service for Christ.

WHEN DOES A BELIEVER RECEIVE THE HOLY SPIRIT?

I think it appropriate to consider further this important matter of when a born again believer receives the Holy Spirit. I start from the point that the epistles in the New Testament never ever refer to a Christian who does not have the indwelling Holy Spirit. This is the case even at Corinth where some believers were involved in very un-Christlike practices yet, as regards having the Holy Spirit, Paul does not distinguish between the believers there. For example, in 1 Corinthians 6:19 he writes:

"know ye not that your body is the temple of the Holy Ghost which is in you, which ye have of God..."

As far as possession of the Holy Spirit is concerned, they were all the same.

When writing to the Ephesians, if we take 1:13-14 and 4:30 together, Paul writes that, having believed,

"ye were sealed with that holy Spirit of promise, which is the earnest of our inheritance ... sealed unto the day of redemption."

The Spirit is the earnest or *guarantee* of what we have in Christ. He is God's seal to confirm that we have received the Gospel of our salvation. If we don't have the Spirit, we aren't sealed. If we aren't sealed, we don't belong to Christ. Dear Christian reader, don't strive to receive the Holy Spirit because, as a Christian, you already have Him!

A time of change

I think some of the confusion on this matter arises because we forget the background to the Acts to which reference was made earlier. The book of the Acts represents a time of transition before the New Testament was written. It was also a time when God was demonstrating to the Jews that the Gospel of His grace is to all people on the basis of faith in Christ alone and this would be hard for some Jews to accept. Accordingly, after Pentecost in Acts 2, there are three other recorded instances in the book when the Holy Spirit comes into believers.

1.   In Acts 8:14-17, believers in *Samaria* received the Spirit when the apostles Peter and John laid their hands on them.

2.   In Acts 10:44-48, the Spirit fell on the first Christian *Gentiles* in Cæsarea as the apostle Peter spoke to them; verse 45 records that the Jews who had become Christians and were present on that occasion "were astonished … because that on the Gentiles also was poured out the gift of the Holy Ghost."

3.   In Acts 19:1-7, in Ephesus Paul found some believers who may previously have been disciples of John the Baptist but who certainly had been *baptised to John's baptism*. Paul the apostle laid his hands on them and they received the Holy Spirit.

Incidentally, *the Holy Spirit* and *the Holy Ghost* are terms used to describe the same Person.

At that time of change, God was sending out important messages to the Jews. The Jews and the Samaritans just did not get on. In Acts 8, there was a public demonstration to the Jews that Jews and Samaritans who believe in Christ are both indwelt by the same Holy Spirit. Jews could never have imagined that Gentiles who believed in Christ would have precisely the same position as Jews who believed in Christ. In Acts 10 they were being taught clearly that that is precisely the case and were astonished at the lesson. John the Baptist was a great man in the eyes of the Jews and in Acts 19 they were shown that John and his baptism merely pointed forwards towards Christ, that Christ is whom all believers follow and that the Holy Spirit indwells all believers. These Scriptures in Acts provide no support at all for the notion that a believer receives the Spirit at some later stage after conversion. If they did, they would contradict the clear message of the epistles and the Bible, God's Word, is incapable of contradiction. There was only one Pentecost at which the Spirit came to indwell all the believers, and subsequently immediately on the conversion of any Christian.

"Having" and "being filled"

I should point out the difference between *having the Spirit*, which is a one-off event which took place at Pentecost and subsequently occurs on conversion, and *being filled with the Spirit*. More than once, both Peter and Paul were described as being filled with the Spirit which therefore is a constant challenge to each believer to allow the Spirit to take control of their lives so that the fruit of the Spirit can be seen. At Pentecost, *having* and *being filled* occurred simultaneously – see 2:2-4.

Pentecost is a great subject and fundamental to Christian teaching. The church was formed then. The Holy Spirit, as great a Person as Christ, came to dwell in every believer, never on this earth to leave them, always to be alongside them, guide them into the truth and give them the power to live for Christ. Pentecost was truly a key event, not just in the Acts, but in the whole of God's dealings with man.

Today, as believers in our Lord Jesus Christ, let us rejoice in the fact that we are indeed indwelt by the Holy Spirit. Never let us lose the wonder of this fact – the Holy Spirit of God, the One co-equal with the Father and the Son in the triune God, actually lives inside the youngest believer in Christ. Let us so live in the power that He brings that our lives are Christ-like and Christ-honouring!

Mark 6

Our subject is chapter 6 of the Gospel of Mark. Before looking into our chapter, it is important to remind ourselves of some general features of Mark's Gospel. Mark presents Jesus as the *Servant* compared with Jesus as *King* in Matthew, as the *Son of Man* in Luke and as the *Son of God* in John. Mark's is the shortest of the four Gospels as things move quickly, in keeping with the constant action of a servant and the frequent use of words such as "straightway" and "immediately". Unlike the other Gospels, there is no earthly or heavenly genealogy in Mark because the test of a servant is not his background but his ability actually to do the job well. Chapter 1 introduces Jesus, emphasising that, though a Servant, He is the Son of God.

Mark's Gospel contains far more miracles than parables – more actions than words – in keeping with this presentation of Jesus as a Servant. In chapter 5 there are three of those miracles, demonstrating the power of Jesus over demons, disease and death. Chapter 6 contains further miracles in the second half but deals with a range of other matters in the first half. There are seven sections in this chapter:

verses 1-6	Jesus in His home area of Nazareth;
verses 7-13	the twelve disciples sent out to preach;
verses 14-29	King Herod's reaction to Jesus and details of Herod's murder of John the Baptist;
verses 30-31	the twelve disciples report back to Jesus;
verses 32-44	the feeding of the 5,000;
verses 45-52	Jesus walks on the water;
verses 53-56	Jesus heals in the land of Gennesaret.

I would like to touch on each of those seven sections and in particular to point to something of what each teaches of Jesus the perfect Servant and to see, where relevant, what we Christians, as His servants, can learn from Him.

JESUS IN HIS HOME AREA OF NAZARETH (VERSES 1-6)

The first six verses record the Lord's return to Nazareth where He was brought up. The locals knew of His humble origins and could not accept that the astonishing things which He taught in the synagogue demonstrated that Jesus had divine origins and was not just a working class man. They had been favoured with His presence but they had no faith to see beyond His outward appearance. Parts of verses 5 and 6 record that Jesus

> "could there do no mighty work, save that he laid
> his hands upon a few sick folk, and healed them.
> And he marvelled because of their unbelief."

It wasn't that Jesus had no capability to do mighty works. The emphasis is on the need for faith which was completely lacking in those who lived at Nazareth. Jesus left Nazareth and the Gospels do not indicate that He ever returned there. A solemn warning to those who reject Jesus!

THE TWELVE DISCIPLES SENT OUT TO PREACH (VERSES 7-13)

Verse 7 says:

> "And he called unto him the twelve, and began to send them forth by two and two".

This is an important point in time. Up to this point, Jesus Himself had preached. Now He was sending out others who could pass on His message. These men had first spent time with Jesus, had seen His actions as the perfect Servant, had been taught by Him, for example through the parables contained in chapter 4, and had seen His power displayed in the mighty miracles. Now they as His servants were to go out in the service of heaven. In verses 8-12 Jesus gives them instructions as to how to go about their service, not relying on natural support, not risking upsetting anyone by moving lodgings, and looking for faith in the hearers.

Here is some guidance for us as the Lord's servants today. Before extensive outward service we must spend time with Jesus, studying His word to learn about the truth contained in Him. As Jesus sent out His disciples, so we need to allow Him to direct our service for Him. Jesus emphasises the value of fellowship in service by sending out the disciples in twos. Jesus could do all by Himself; we need the support of our fellow-believers. The resources for our service are not our own wealth or status. And we must be discerning, wise and thoughtful in all that we do.

KING HEROD'S REACTION TO JESUS AND DETAILS OF HEROD'S MURDER OF JOHN THE BAPTIST (VERSES 14-29)

Let's read verses 14-18:

> "And king Herod heard of him; (for his name was spread abroad:) and he said, That John the Baptist was risen from the dead, and therefore mighty works do shew forth themselves in him. Others said, That it is Elias. And others said, That it is a prophet, or as one of the prophets. But when Herod heard thereof, he said, It is John, whom I beheaded: he is risen from the dead. For Herod himself had sent forth and laid hold upon John, and bound him in prison for Herodias' sake, his brother Philip's wife: for he had married her. For John had said unto Herod, It is not lawful for thee to have thy brother's wife."

The remainder of the verses in this section fill in details of Herod's murder of John the Baptist.

This section takes up a considerable proportion of the chapter – around a quarter of it. Why should such emphasis be given to this matter? I can only suggest that a possible answer is found in the position of these verses. The disciples had just been sent out in their service for Jesus. I suggest that these verses indicate the nature of the audience to whom they will preach. John the Baptist had not flinched from sticking to the truth and consistently telling Herod that he was breaking Old Testament law in taking his brother's wife. Ultimately Herod was responsible for the murder of John as these verses in this section set out. Herod placed more importance on keeping face with those who had heard his foolish promise to a young girl than to adhering to

God's requirements. Now Herod's conscience was troubling him as he recalled all this.

The Lord's servants then and now go out to preach and serve in a world which does not place God or His Word as the topmost consideration. 2 Timothy 3:2-5 warns that

> "men shall be lovers of their own selves, … boasters, proud, … unholy, … despisers of those that are good, … lovers of pleasures more than lovers of God …".

These things applied to Herod and generally apply today. Men and women do have a conscience but as with Herod there is often the inclination to ignore the message of conscience and to give most attention to that which gratifies self. God does not take first place. That is the feature of the world in which the Lord's servants seek to serve Him.

THE TWELVE DISCIPLES REPORT BACK TO JESUS (VERSES 30-31)

Verses 30-31 comprise the fourth section of our chapter.

> "And the apostles gathered themselves together unto Jesus, and told him all things, both what they had done, and what they had taught. And he said unto them, Come ye yourselves apart into a desert place, and rest a while: for there were many coming and going, and they had no leisure so much as to eat."

I think that these are lovely verses! Having preached and served among those who generally would not have put God's things in first place, the disciples report back to Jesus and tell Him everything about their service. The Lord takes them apart with Himself into a place of quietness, away from all the hustle and bustle of service, to spend time alone with Him so that He can ensure that they are fed on what will build them up again for fresh service.

What a joy it is to talk to Jesus about our service for Him; to tell Him of all the encouragements and disappointments. Of course He already knows all about it but He wants us to keep reporting back. It is also essential to take time out in His presence, alone with Him to allow Him to feed us. Do you find, dear Christian, as I do, that the constant rush, the "coming and going" of verse 31, can result in this quality time with Jesus being minimised? Yet the Lord emphasises the need for this time, where He can speak to me; to encourage me when I'm disappointed, if necessary to keep things in balance, and remind me, when I may be elated, that He is the only source of success and, generally, to build me up. An important lesson for every servant of the Lord!

THE FEEDING OF THE 5,000 (VERSES 32-44)

This brings us to the fifth section of the chapter and I would like us to read the whole of this section:

> "And they departed into a desert place by ship privately. And the people saw them departing, and many knew him, and ran afoot thither out of all cities, and outwent them, and came together unto him. And Jesus, when he came out, saw much people, and was moved with compassion toward them, because they were as sheep not having a shepherd: and he began to teach them many things. And when the day was now far spent, his disciples came unto him, and said, This is a desert place, and now the time is far passed: Send them away, that they may go into the country round about, and into the villages, and buy themselves

bread: for they have nothing to eat. He answered
and said unto them, Give ye them to eat. And they
say unto him, Shall we go and buy two hundred
pennyworth of bread, and give them to eat? He
saith unto them, How many loaves have ye? go
and see. And when they knew, they say, Five, and
two fishes. And he commanded them to make all
sit down by companies upon the green grass. And
they sat down in ranks, by hundreds, and by
fifties. And when he had taken the five loaves and
the two fishes, he looked up to heaven, and
blessed, and brake the loaves, and gave them to his
disciples to set before them; and the two fishes
divided he among them all. And they did all eat,
and were filled. And they took up twelve baskets
full of the fragments, and of the fishes. And they
that did eat of the loaves were about five thousand
men."

This is the only miracle recorded in all four of the
Gospels and therefore has a special message for us. As
mentioned at the beginning, each Gospel presents the
Lord Jesus in a different aspect. It seems to me that,
whichever aspect of the Lord is being presented, the
Holy Spirit inspired each Gospel writer to include this
miracle so as to emphasise that there is a super-abun-
dance available then and now in Jesus.

Service based on love

I want to draw your attention first of all to verse 34.
Jesus had been looking to take His disciples to a quiet
place, to spend time alone with Him. On arrival, instead
of quietness there was "much people". Was Jesus
annoyed or did He ignore them and go elsewhere? Not
a bit of it! This verse records the perfect action of the

perfect Servant in that He "was moved with compassion toward them". If my service is not based on love to those whom I serve, I don't have the right to expect blessing. This love is not just some superficial feeling but a deep movement of my heart, as was the case with Jesus.

Based on that movement of love, Jesus then taught them. He provided for their spiritual needs before looking after their bodily needs. He did both, but the order is important. In the world around us, many are lost and don't know the Good Shepherd. The most urgent need is for men and women to be pointed to Jesus so that their souls can be eternally satisfied.

Only one hope

Then, the disciples made a natural but fundamental error. They and the crowd were in a desert place with no food available. Instead of recognising that the only hope of providing food in this place was Jesus, they urged the Lord to send the people away. In another Gospel (John 6:68), Peter the disciple is recorded as saying,

> "Lord, to whom shall we go? thou hast the words of eternal life."

Dear fellow-believer, do we really fully comprehend that our Saviour Jesus is the only One who can save people from their sins and secure them a place in heaven? The same Peter is recorded in Acts 4:12 as saying:

> "Neither is there salvation in any other: for there is none other name under heaven given among men, whereby we must be saved."

We can't send people away to anyone else because there is nobody else to help.

Gifts for service

Then the disciples identify that all they had to feed this great crowd were five loaves and two fish. In the Bible, five often speaks of human weakness and limitation, for example the five fingers and five toes which we have. The fact that there were five loaves emphasises the inability of the disciples and others to meet the great need. But the key here is that the small number of loaves and fish were brought to Jesus, and He took them and He used them for such immense blessing.

Do you ever feel that the gifts which you have for the Lord's service are so small that they are not much use in the context of the great need around? I certainly feel that about myself. The key is to bring those gifts to Jesus and let Him take them and use them, sometimes in a way in which we could never imagine. I have no doubt that Jesus could have turned the stones in this desert place into bread, but Jesus chose to use what was brought to Him. It seems to me that this remains the pattern, that Jesus chooses to work through His servants and can use any gift fully placed into His hands.

Order and comfort

Let us also notice that the service of the perfect Servant was an orderly one. The people were made to sit down in manageable groups. His service was not haphazard, rushing from one thing to another. It was undertaken with thought and care and I conclude that my service for the Lord should be similarly characterised. Note also that the presence of the Lord brings comfort; the people sat down on "the green grass". It reminds me of David's words in Psalm 23:2:

"He maketh me to lie down in green pastures".

Source and supply

Having taken the loaves and fish, the first thing Jesus does is to look up to heaven and bless the loaves and fish. The perfect Servant draws attention away from Himself and points to heaven as the source of blessing. This is a salutary lesson for all servants of the Lord. Never should we seek to draw attention to ourselves. When there is blessing, it arises not from the servant but from God in heaven.

Finally, look at how much Jesus provided from the small amount given to Him. Verse 42 tells us that all of this big crowd were filled. Not only that, but twelve baskets were filled with the scraps left over. In my job, arithmetic is important and I note in this miracle that the rules of arithmetic are broken. We start with something, take away more than we started with and are left with more than we started with! But in this miracle we are dealing with a Person who is not limited by anything. He can still provide unlimited blessing in any circumstances. This world is like a desert and has nothing to help men and women in the real needs of their souls but Jesus can give eternal life, something not limited by anything in this world, not even by death.

JESUS WALKS ON THE WATER (VERSES 45-52)

Mark introduces the sixth section of this chapter by one of his typical phrases: "And straightway". A servant is always quickly on the move from one situation to another.

Here, Jesus, having dealt with the spiritual and physical needs of the people, sends them home. He instructs His disciples to get into the boat and go to the other side of Galilee. In the meantime, Jesus went into a mountain to pray. After the noteworthy miracle and despite having a very heavy day of teaching and activity, this perfect Servant found it essential to spend time in prayer. What an example to us! Communion with God in prayer is vital for servants of the Lord at all times. Remove the times in prayer and we don't have the power and direction in service. If Jesus as a Man and a Servant needed to spend time in prayer, how much more do I?

While Jesus was praying, the disciples were in the boat on the Sea of Galilee, struggling to row against the difficult wind. Seas in Scripture often speak of the world around us, never still, often causing difficulties. Like the disciples in the boat, Christians have been put in a separate place but are still subject to the problems and difficulties around and we often find it hard to move against these factors. Jesus demonstrated His control over natural elements, first of all by walking on the water and moving more quickly than the boat, despite the disciples' combined efforts at rowing. Then the wind ceased, surely not by coincidence but by the influence of Jesus when He came into the boat.

In our service and in our lives we as Christians are often subject to contrary and difficult situations. It is only when we call Jesus into those situations that we can find any peace. Battling against the problems in our own strength gets us nowhere. Jesus wants to come on board, directly alongside in the problem situation to uplift and help us with those lovely words from verse 50:

"Be of good cheer: it is I; be not afraid."

One final little suggestion on this section. Verse 48 says that Jesus came on board in the problems of "the fourth watch of the night" – the hours just before dawn. 2 Peter 1:19 talks about

"… a light that shineth in a dark place, until the day dawn, and the day star arise in your hearts".

Surely the second coming of Jesus is drawing near when He will come as the day star for His people. The Bible teaches that, as that day draws near, as it were in the fourth and final watch of the night, things in the world will get worse, and in these trying times Jesus wants to be on board and to cheer us and help us with His presence.

JESUS HEALS IN THE LAND OF GENNESARET (VERSES 53-56)

The final section of our chapter takes place in the land of Gennesaret, which I understand is at the north west edge of the Sea of Galilee. These verses record that there was great excitement as Jesus arrived and He undertook much healing. Those who had the faith to touch even the hem of His garment were made well. Of course, the power for healing was not in the garment but in the One who wore it! At the beginning of Mark 6 in Nazareth, lack of faith caused Jesus to leave that area. At the end of the chapter, faith among those living in Gennesaret brought blessing to that area. Personal faith in Jesus is crucial!

One of the joys in preparing these messages is the pleasure gained in prayerful consideration of the particular Bible verses, especially when Jesus so clearly is the subject of the verses. Those readers who are Christians, I trust that you will join me in trying the more to copy the example of the perfect Servant as we seek to serve God. If any reading do not know Jesus as their Saviour, I do urge you to put your faith in Him and only in Him. Jesus is not only the perfect Servant; He is also the great Saviour.

The power of God's word – Jonah 3

SERIES: LESSONS FROM THE LIFE OF JONAH

BROADCAST DATE: 8TH MARCH 2009

Before turning to Jonah 3, it may be useful briefly to summarise the earlier part of the life of Jonah. Jonah is first mentioned in the Bible in 2 Kings 14:25 from where we learn that Jonah's father was Amittai and that he was born in Gathhepher, which I understand is in Galilee, not far from Nazareth. It is not clear exactly when Jonah lived but it is likely to have been about 800 or 900 BC.

RUNNING AWAY FROM GOD (JONAH 1)

Jonah was instructed by God to go to the great Assyrian city of Nineveh and to warn of God's judgement against the people of that city because of their wickedness. Instead of obeying God, he went by ship in the opposite direction, trying to flee from God's presence. God prepared a great storm and the sailors were much afraid, knowing that Jonah was disobeying God. Jonah told the sailors to throw him overboard and then the seas were calm. The sailors turned to God.

CAN THERE BE FORGIVENESS? (JONAH 2)

God had not forgotten Jonah despite his disobedience. In His grace, God prepared a great fish which swallowed Jonah. He was there for three days and three nights. Jonah's earnest prayer from the belly of the great fish is recorded in chapter 2. Nowhere in the Bible can a prayer have been made from a more unusual place! Jonah repented, the Lord heard his prayer and Jonah is recorded in verse 9 as saying "Salvation is of the LORD." Jonah's change had begun and God, who always hears a genuine prayer of repentance, caused the great fish to vomit out Jonah on dry land. An almost unbelievable story but one which is authenticated by the Lord Jesus Himself in Matthew 12 and Luke 11.

A SECOND CHANCE

This brings us to Jonah 3, and our title is "The power of God's word".

During the course of this study we will read the whole of Jonah 3. We'll start by reading from the beginning of verse 1 to the middle of verse 3:

> "And the word of the LORD came unto Jonah the second time, saying, Arise, go unto Nineveh, that great city, and preach unto it the preaching that I bid thee. So Jonah arose, and went unto Nineveh, according to the word of the LORD."

What a change has now taken place in God's servant, Jonah! God's instruction to His servant hadn't changed and His message hadn't changed. However, *Jonah* certainly had changed because of God's dealings with him. In chapter 1, Jonah's response to God's instruction was complete disobedience combined with the folly of thinking that he could run away from the presence of

God, the One who is omnipresent. Here, in contrast, in chapter 3 Jonah's obedience to God's repeated instruction is immediate.

THREE LESSONS FOR SERVANTS

From these first few verses of Jonah 3, I would like to take three lessons for all of us who, like Jonah, would be servants of God.

The servant learns the ways of God

The first lesson is that being a servant of God is a *learning* process which I believe continues throughout a servant's life. Never is a servant so knowledgeable or so advanced that he or she has nothing further to learn. Jonah had to be taken to rock bottom before his spiritual education could proceed. From the belly of the great fish he proclaimed: "Salvation is of the LORD." In other words, this servant, Jonah, had learned in dramatic circumstances that he was nothing in himself but everything proceeded from God. From that realisation, God could now re-instruct His servant.

However, Jonah was not yet the finished article. Chapter 4 teaches us that the servant Jonah still had much to learn from God. At the beginning of chapter 3, Jonah was a more useable servant than at the beginning of the book, but he still had much to learn. How important it is really to take note and learn from the way that God speaks to us! For most of us, God's way of speaking is likely to be far less dramatic than in the case of Jonah, but God wants us to learn so that we are of more use to Him. I ask myself, how readily am I learning?

The servant obeys the instructions of God

The second lesson I would like to take from the beginning of Jonah 3 is the matter of *obedience*. The crucial aspect of obedience is underlined for us right from the beginning of the Bible. In Genesis 3 sin enters the world because of disobedience against a specific and straight-forward instruction of God. In the face of King Saul's disobedience to God, in 1 Samuel 15:22, Samuel states that:

> "Behold, to obey is better than sacrifice, and to hearken than the fat of rams."

It was only when Jesus came into this world, that someone could truly say, as Jesus did, in John 15:10:

> "I have kept my Father's commandments".

Jonah had to learn that obedience to God is critical. If a servant obeys God's instructions, blessing will result – as it does later in our chapter. We are not asked to question but to obey. In Acts 8:6 & 26, Philip the evangelist was being greatly blessed in Samaria but God instructed him to move from there to a desert place in the south. What reason could there be for this? But Philip did not question God's instruction. Immediately he obeyed and in that desert place an important man from Ethiopia was converted and baptised. Obedience on the part of Philip resulted in blessing. Later, in Acts 16:6-9, Paul and his companions were journeying westwards, not sure exactly where to go and only wanting to go where the Lord instructed. Eventually the Lord spoke to them and in verse 10 of that chapter it says that

> "... immediately we endeavoured to go into Macedonia, assuredly gathering that the Lord had called us for to preach the gospel unto them."

Paul obeyed and there was great blessing in Macedonia with the first preaching of the gospel in Europe.

And what about me? Do I seek always to obey God's word – the Bible – in every respect? That is what God wants above everything else. My responsibility is first to Him, not first to anybody or anything else. Jonah didn't *want* to go to Nineveh, but it was precisely that place where God wanted him to go. Through staying close to the Lord, I can learn His instructions for me regarding service for Him. Sometimes these instructions can be quite specific, as in Jonah's case. Perhaps I may need to take time to see what the instructions for service really are; and sometimes the instructions may start with telling me what *not* to do, as was the case with Paul in Acts 16:6. Sometimes the instructions may seem to go against natural reasoning as may have been the case with Philip in Acts 8. But always for those who set their mind prayerfully to seek God's instructions, I am convinced that He will make His mind known. And ultimately, obedience to God will result in blessing in God's timing.

The servant preaches the Word of God

The last of the three points I want to take from these early verses of Jonah 3 is that Jonah's preaching had to be of *the message given to him by God*; as verse 2 puts it:

> "… go unto Nineveh … and preach unto it the preaching that I bid thee."

Jonah wasn't asked to like or dislike the message. He wasn't expected to over- or under-emphasise various parts of the message according to his own inclination. The message was the word of the LORD, not the word of Jonah, and the servant had to pass it on exactly as he received it from God.

In this day, what the servant of God has to preach should be wholly based on the Word of God – the Bible.

It sometimes seems to me that it is judged up-to-date to pick and choose those parts of the Bible which will be emphasised and to put into the background those parts which are difficult to explain or thought to be less acceptable to the listeners. Right at the end of the Bible there is a very solemn warning to any who either add to or take away from the message of the Bible – see Revelation 22:19.

So, today, any Christian preaching has to be Bible-based. For example, if I am preaching the Gospel, I have to tell it as God tells it in the Bible: that everyone is a sinner, that God is holy and requires a penalty for my sin; that God also is love and gave His Son Jesus to pay the penalty for my sin; that the only way to heaven is by faith in the blood of Jesus; and that Jesus rose from the dead to demonstrate the eternal life that He gives to each person who truly believes in Him. Paul wrote, in 2 Timothy 3:15, that it is

> "*the holy scriptures*, which are able to make thee wise unto salvation through faith which is in Christ Jesus."

Next we will be reading the remainder of Jonah 3, which demonstrates the power of the Word of God which Jonah preached in Nineveh. Of course, God can use His word in power in whatever way He chooses, irrespective of the preacher or the circumstances. But it seems to me that for the servant of God, then or now, this chapter sets out the pattern of blessing which the servant should follow: first, the servant *learns* the ways of God, the servant *obeys* the instructions of God and the servant *preaches* the word of God, and then *God adds His blessing.*

NINEVEH

Now, let"s move on and read the second half of verse 3:

> "Now Nineveh was an exceeding great city of three days' journey."

Just a word about Nineveh, the place to which Jonah was sent to preach God's word. The vast majority of the Old Testament prophets brought God's message to the Jews. But Jonah, a Jew himself, was sent to a Gentile city and would take with him his Jewish prejudices about the Gentiles, quite happy to preach God's wrath against the Gentiles but not so happy to see God forgive people who were not Jews.

Nineveh is first mentioned in Genesis 10:11. It was built by the same family who built Babel and those two cities had a history of self-sufficiency and opposition to God. As we have read, by the time of Jonah Nineveh was a huge city, taking three days to travel round it, and having more than 120,000 young children according to the last verse of Jonah. It was the capital city of Assyria. The attitude of the people of Nineveh is summed up in Zephaniah 2:13-15, where in verse 15 it says that their proud view of themselves was: "I am, and there is none beside me." It was to this place that Jonah was sent with the message of God's judgement. Incidentally, if you have time to read the short Bible book of Nahum, who lived later than Jonah, you will find that it deals exclusively with the prophecy of the ultimate destruction of Nineveh.

GOD ADDS HIS BLESSING

Let's now read the remainder of Jonah 3, starting from verse 4:

"And Jonah began to enter into the city a day's journey, and he cried, and said, Yet forty days, and Nineveh shall be overthrown. So the people of Nineveh believed God, and proclaimed a fast, and put on sackcloth, from the greatest of them even to the least of them. For word came unto the king of Nineveh, and he arose from his throne, and he laid his robe from him, and covered him with sackcloth, and sat in ashes. And he caused it to be proclaimed and published through Nineveh by the decree of the king and his nobles, saying, Let neither man nor beast, herd nor flock, taste anything: let them not feed, nor drink water: but let man and beast be covered with sackcloth, and cry mightily unto God: yea, let them turn every one from his evil way, and from the violence that is in their hands. Who can tell if God will turn and repent, and turn away from his fierce anger, that we perish not? And God saw their works, that they turned from their evil way; and God repented of the evil, that he had said that he would do unto them; and he did it not."

From these verses we see that as soon as Jonah arrived at Nineveh he did not delay in proclaiming the message which God had given him to preach. This must have been real open air preaching! Jonah preached as he journeyed into the city, his message one of judgement from God which would strike the city in forty days' time. The message had an immediate impact as in verse 5 it states that "the people of Nineveh believed God". And this faith in God applied throughout the inhabitants, from the greatest to the least. Their turning to God in faith was evidenced outwardly by their fasting and clothing themselves in sackcloth, including the king (verse 6). It was a time of conversion as people turned from their "evil way" (verses 8 & 10) and turned to God. And God in His grace saw their repentance and did not bring His judgement upon them (verse 10).

May I remind you that our subject is "The power of God's word"? What a demonstration of that power in this chapter! It was the bringing of God's word to that city which brought about this dramatic change in the inhabitants and in their prospects. None of the credit for the change rests with Jonah; he was just the messenger. It was the message, God's word, which brought about the change.

Now all of this happened not too far short of 3,000 years ago. One of the great benefits of studying the Old Testament is that we can see from it God's principles of working and note that those general principles don't change over time. So today it is God's word that still has the power to change lives dramatically. Preachers come and preachers go, political systems and social systems change over time,

> "But the word of the Lord endureth for ever. And this is the word which by the gospel is preached unto you" (1 Peter 1:25).

God's word with its power to change lives is enshrined in the Gospel. Just as at Nineveh, God's word, the Gospel, is preached today with the background of a warning about God's future judgement to come. At Nineveh, the warning was that God's judgement would come in forty days. In the Bible, periods of forty days or years are not too unusual and I think that 40 in the Bible is generally accepted as representing a period of full testing of responsibility. We don't know when God's judgement will fall on this world but it certainly will and at a time when God determines that man has had a full testing of his responsibility to God. Again as at Nineveh, the only way of not suffering God's judgement is by an individual repenting of his or her own sin and turning to God in faith in Him and His word.

If the warning of impending judgement is the background to the preaching of God's word in the Gospel, the *good news* of the Gospel is that God in His love has poured out His judgement on Jesus when He died on the cross; and for anybody who repents of his sin and believes on Jesus as Saviour and Lord, God gives the gift of eternal life. The wonder of this message is summed up in the lovely verse in John 3:16:

> "For God so loved the world, that he gave his only begotten Son, that whosoever believeth in him should not perish, but have everlasting life."

The prospect of God's judgement is terrible; the prospect for anyone who has everlasting life is terrific.

REPENTANCE

Jonah 3 emphasises the importance for the people of Nineveh of repentance. Perhaps we don't always sufficiently stress the importance of repentance toward God in our Gospel preachings today. Repentance is vital, and is no light matter of saying sorry in a superficial way. Repentance involves me recognising that God abhors sin, and that I am a sinner and my sin is against a holy God. Conversion involves a deep, deep sense of the awfulness of my sin and a life-changing turning away from it in repentance. As with the people of Nineveh, God sees that repentance and in His grace removes the judgement which my sin deserved.

Let us also remember that the people of Nineveh evidenced their repentance and faith toward God by a change in their behaviour. My conversion to Christ should result in a change of my way of life which should be evident to those around. This is illustrated so often in the four Gospels as the lives of people are completely changed by Jesus. One of the most dramatic illustrations is in the case of Legion in the first part of Mark 5, where that untamed man, who spent his time in the mountains and graveyards crying and cutting himself, met Jesus and by verse 15 of that chapter was with Jesus "sitting, and clothed, and in his right mind".

Dear reader, every conversion to Christ is a triumphant evidence of the power of God's word to change lives. The challenge to me as a Christian is whether I show that inward change by the outward evidence of a changed life.

One final thought: the generation of inhabitants of Nineveh described in Jonah 3 repented and turned in faith to God. Sadly, history tells us that later generations in Nineveh did not follow God but returned to the sinful ways of the generations which preceded Jonah's preaching. God's judgement then fell on Nineveh, which history tells us was destroyed, as prophesied by Nahum. It is for *individuals* in each generation to repent and turn in faith to God. The personal faith of individuals in a past generation is an example, but is of no value before God for individuals in a succeeding generation. In Britain, we are blest to have many fine examples of Christians who lived here in past generations. Each of us *now* has to decide *for ourselves* whether to turn to God in personal saving faith.

NOT ASHAMED OF THE GOSPEL

I want us to be left with a clear impression of the undiminished power of God's word, both in Jonah's day and now, to change lives and situations. The Word of God is the basis of the life-changing Gospel of the grace of God. As Paul wrote, in Romans 1:16,

> "For I am not ashamed of the gospel of Christ: for it is the power of God unto salvation to every one that believeth; …"

A glorious Saviour – Mark 9

SERIES: GOD'S SERVANT IN MARK'S GOSPEL

BROADCAST DATE: 12TH JULY 2009

Before turning to Mark 9, it is important to remind ourselves of some general features of Mark's Gospel. Mark presents Jesus as the *Servant* compared with Jesus as *King* in Matthew, as *Son of Man* in Luke and as the *Son of God* in John. Mark's is the shortest of the four Gospels as things move quickly, in keeping with the constant action of a servant and the frequent use of words such as "straightway" and "immediately". Unlike the other Gospels, there is no earthly or heavenly genealogy in Mark because the test of a servant is not his background but his ability actually to do the job well. Chapter 1 introduces Jesus, emphasising that, though a Servant, He is the Son of God. Mark's Gospel contains far more miracles than parables – more actions than words – in keeping with this presentation of Jesus as a Servant.

Our subject is "A glorious Saviour". In the immediately preceding chapters, Jesus had been performing miracles in the area around the Sea of Galilee and He continues in that area throughout chapter 9. I would like to divide this chapter into three sections:

verses 1-13 the transfiguration;

verses 14-29 Jesus casting out a demon from a child;

verses 30-50 the Lord talks to His disciples.

THE TRANSFIGURATION (VERSES 1-13)

Verse 1 of our chapter strictly belongs to the events and words of chapter 8. However, it is also a link verse to chapter 9.

> "And he (Jesus) said unto them, Verily I say unto you, That there be some of them that stand here, which shall not taste of death, till they have seen the kingdom of God come with power."

Here Jesus was foretelling that in a few days' time three of His disciples would actually see a foretaste of the kingdom of God. I don't imagine that any of those listening understood what the Lord meant or the privilege to be granted to some individuals to witness the power of God to bring this event to pass. Now we must read verses 2-13:

> "And after six days Jesus taketh with him Peter, and James, and John, and leadeth them up into an high mountain apart by themselves: and he was transfigured before them. And his raiment became shining, exceeding white as snow; so as no fuller on earth can white them. And there appeared unto them Elias with Moses: and they were talking with Jesus. And Peter answered and said to Jesus, Master, it is good for us to be here: and let us make three tabernacles; one for thee, and one for Moses, and one for Elias. For he wist

not what to say; for they were sore afraid. And there was a cloud that overshadowed them: and a voice came out of the cloud, saying, This is my beloved Son: hear him. And suddenly, when they had looked round about, they saw no man any more, save Jesus only with themselves. And as they came down from the mountain, he charged them that they should tell no man what things they had seen, till the Son of man were risen from the dead. And they kept that saying with themselves, questioning one with another what the rising from the dead should mean. And they asked him, saying, Why say the scribes that Elias must first come? And he answered and told them, Elias verily cometh first, and restoreth all things; and how it is written of the Son of man, that he must suffer many things, and be set at nought. But I say unto you, That Elias is indeed come, and they have done unto him whatsoever they listed, as it is written of him."

This is an amazing event! What is its purpose? Shortly we will consider some of the detail, but I believe that one of the main purposes of the record of the transfiguration is to present a prophecy that Jesus will, at some stage in the future, return in His great glory to establish His kingdom on this earth for the period that is generally referred to as the Millennium, and that His saints will return with Him.

The transfiguration is also recorded in Matthew 17 and in Luke 9. If you have time and are interested in studying the Bible, a comparison of the detail of these three records of the transfiguration is an interesting and rewarding exercise. The reasons for many differences between these records can be traced back to the different presentations of the Lord in the various Gospels, as I referred to earlier. The transfiguration is not recorded in John's Gospel and I suggest the reason for this could be that John emphasises the Person of the Son of God rather than His glory to be seen on earth.

Moving into the detail in Mark 9: Peter, James and John saw Jesus "transfigured before them" (verse 2). This word *transfigured* literally means 'to change into another form'. I understand that the word used is the same as the basis for metamorphosis which is used in a zoological sense as the term to describe the complete and dramatic change between the immature form and the adult form of some animals. The change in the Lord's form was also dramatic and these men actually saw the Lord's glory shining out.

Mark's emphasis in verse 3 is on the Lord's *clothing* which he describes as shining or dazzling, and not just white, but exceeding white like the whiteness of pure snow, whiter than anyone in the world could bleach them. Do you get a sense that Mark is struggling for human words which will adequately describe this scene of glory where all the focus is on this glorious Saviour?

Both Matthew and Luke record that the Lord's *face* or *countenance* shone – shone "as the sun", as it says in Matthew 17:2. Mark emphasises the Lord's clothing because it is that which is seen outwardly and Mark continues to bring Jesus as the Servant to our attention. How unusual to equate a servant with glory but here in Jesus is the Servant who was perfect and glorious in everything that He did.

Then in verse 4, the three disciples see two Old Testament men of God talking with the transfigured Jesus. There is Elijah, sometimes referred to as the servant prophet, and there is Moses, used by God to give the law. As we know, Elijah was taken out of this world to heaven while still alive. Moses died and was buried. Sometimes these two Old Testament men are suggested as representative of groups of saints, Elijah of saints who are *alive* when Jesus comes and who go to heaven without dying and Moses of saints who have *died* but whom Jesus will raise.

The disciples were afraid at what they saw. The record brings us back down to earth because Peter, as impulsive as usual, says that they should make three tabernacles or booths for the three men they had just seen. He effectively was making Jesus, Elijah and Moses all of equal standing. This is the same Peter who only in the previous chapter had declared to Jesus that "Thou art the Christ" – God's chosen, unique One.

God moved immediately to speak on this important issue. If we look back to the end of Exodus 40, we see there that when the tabernacle was complete a cloud came over it and verses 34-35 of that chapter tell us that that cloud was equated with the glory of the LORD. It is worth reading again Mark 9:7:

> "And there was a cloud that overshadowed them: and a voice came out of the cloud, saying, This is my beloved Son: hear him."

The disciples had just seen a display of glory on the mountain. Now, in keeping with that, a cloud signifying God's glory overshadowed them and God's voice spoke to them to remind them that God's Son is unique and far above any other person, even two great men like Elijah and Moses. God's voice told them to hear what His Son had to say. It was His Son alone who spoke with absolute authority. May I suggest that this is also a reminder for us today that, whatever anyone else may say, authority rests *only* with what God and His Son say, as recorded in the Bible, the Word of God.

Almost as if to emphasise this, Mark then writes in verse 8 that at this point the disciples looked around and saw nobody else "save Jesus only". People come and people go, but Jesus is always there. God was pointing these men to His Son and what a difference seeing Jesus only could make to their lives and to our lives too!

On the way down the mountain, Jesus instructs the three not to tell anyone what they had seen until Jesus had risen from the dead, or as the accurate translation is, until Jesus had risen from among the dead. The disciples were puzzled about this. They understood and believed the truth of the resurrection of the dead but that an individual should rise from among the dead was beyond their understanding.

Finally in this section of the chapter, probably arising from seeing Elijah on the mountain top, the three disciples ask Jesus about Elijah's relationship to certain events. Jesus confirmed to them that Elijah would first come prior to the Lord's first coming into this world and prior to the Lord's appearing at the end of the Great Tribulation. If we were to look at Matthew 17:11-13, we would see that John the Baptist was sent like an Elijah to precede the first coming of Jesus into this world; that had already happened. Looking to the future, Malachi 4:5-6 states that another one like Elijah will come

> "before the coming of the great and dreadful day of the LORD".

At the time of this conversation in Mark 9, both the sufferings of Jesus at the cross and the coming of another

Elijah-like person lay in the future, but these coming events are certain.

I have taken some time over the first 13 verses in this chapter of 50 verses but this record of the transfiguration with its display of Christ's glory is amazing. When you have time, read 2 Peter 1:16-19, where Peter looks back on the transfiguration. It had left an indelible mark on Peter. In those verses he refers to them being "eye-witnesses of his majesty" and to hearing God's voice of approval of His Son "from the excellent glory". I believe that as we consider the wonders of Jesus, God's Son, by faith we can receive glimpses of His glory – His unique, supreme excellence – and this can transform us in our appreciation *of* Him and of our living *for* Him.

JESUS CASTING OUT A DEMON FROM A CHILD (VERSES 14-29)

We come now to the second section of our chapter. Jesus and the three disciples come down from the glory of the mountain of transfiguration immediately to be confronted by a situation which demonstrated Satan's power and the horror of what happens when that power takes hold of a person. A father had brought his son to the other nine disciples. These verses tell us that, from being a young child, the son had been possessed by an evil spirit which caused him to be deaf and dumb and to have seizures. The convulsions made the son foam at the mouth and grind his teeth. Sometimes the demon cast him into the fire or into water in an attempt to destroy him. The son was wasting away. The father was desperate.

The nine disciples had been unable to do anything and the scribes were making the most of the situation in front of a large crowd of onlookers. The disciples were powerless at this display of the effects of Satanic power.

But then Jesus takes over and calls for the son to be brought to Him.

Initially this seems to make matters worse because, when the demon saw Jesus, he completely convulsed the boy, who fell to the ground, rolling around and foaming at the mouth. Before dealing with the demon, Jesus makes two references to faith, firstly in verse 19 to the *lack* of it in that present generation and then in verses 23-24 to the *need* of the boy's father to have faith if his son was to be healed. It seems from verse 22 that the father was not confident that Jesus had the power to heal, but in verse 24 the tearful father utters from his heart those crucial words "Lord, I believe". In response to that faith, Jesus demonstrated His power over the evil spirit by instructing it to come out of the boy and never to enter him again. At that, the demon had one final surge of power over the lad, leaving him lying on the ground looking as if he was dead. Jesus then helped the son get up and he was fine.

The early chapters of Mark contain many miracles but there are not many after this one. I want to emphasise three points from it.

There is no greater power than the power of Jesus!

The first is to notice that it was only the power of Jesus which could overcome the power of Satan and bring real life where previously there had been a pitiful existence. The disciples were powerless, but the demon had to bow to the authority of Jesus. There is no greater power than the power of Jesus! The Bible teaches that in a day to come that power will be demonstrated on this earth when all the forces of Satan will be defeated and every-one and everything will bow the knee to Jesus. Even today, the power of Jesus over sin is shown whenever someone becomes a Christian. The power of Jesus can change any life and overcome any sin.

The importance of faith in Jesus

The second point I want to underline from this miracle is the importance of faith in Jesus. It was only when the son's father showed that faith that his son's healing took place. The Bible teaches that personal faith in Jesus is required before my sins can be forgiven. As Romans 10:9 tells us, I have to believe in my heart before I can be saved.

The importance of prayer

Thirdly, after the disciples asked Jesus why they could not cast out the demon, Jesus tells them in verse 29 of the importance for His followers of prayer. Prayer demonstrates dependence on divine power. The disciples themselves did not have power but prayer would provide it to them from the One who has all power.

THE LORD TALKS TO HIS DISCIPLES (VERSES 30-50)

So to the last section of Mark 9, in which the Lord is talking to His disciples as they journey together. It seems that there are four matters which He wishes to bring to their attention.

His forthcoming death and resurrection (verses 30-32)

Let's read from verses 31-32:

> "The Son of man is delivered into the hands of men, and they shall kill him; and after that he is killed, he shall rise the third day. But they understood not that saying, and were afraid to ask him."

This was by no means the first time Jesus had told His disciples of these events to come, for example in Mark 8:31, nor was it to be the last. The Lord's words seem clear to us, but for the disciples at that time there was no understanding and they were even afraid to ask Jesus what He meant. Of course they did not at that time have the Holy Spirit abiding in them to reveal the truth of God, but might it also be that their thoughts were taken up with hopes of Jesus very quickly establishing His kingdom on this earth? The idea of Jesus being killed hardly fitted with that prospect.

The divine order of greatness (verses 33-37)

The second matter which Jesus brings to His disciples' attention arises because Jesus knew that the disciples had been arguing amongst themselves which of them would be greatest in the kingdom, which they envisaged Jesus shortly setting up on earth.

In this Gospel which portrays the perfect Servant, Jesus tells His disciples of the divine order of greatness (verse 35):

> "If any man desire to be first, the same shall be last of all, and servant of all."

Later in the Bible, Paul, writing to the Philippians (2:5-7) says:

> "... Christ Jesus ... equal with God ... took upon him(self) the form of a servant ...".

Jesus lived out the taking of a servant's place, despite His greatness. Jesus reinforces His message by taking into His arms a child, an inconsequential being in the normal order of things, and tells them that receiving a child in the name of Jesus, means that the receiver of the child also welcomes Jesus and His Father.

Disciple means 'learner'. The disciples were having to learn some important lessons from the One who is both glorious Saviour and perfect Servant. Each of us also has to learn these lessons from the same Person.

Acting in the name of Jesus and opposing Satan (verses 38-41)

The third of the four matters results directly from what Jesus said in the previous verses. John said that the disciples had rebuked a man who was casting out demons in the name of Jesus and yet was not one of the twelve disciples. That man was doing what these disciples had been unable to do earlier in the chapter. Jesus draws from this the lesson that "he that is not against us is on our part" (verse 40). The crucial thing was that the man was acting in the name of Jesus, and in opposing what was of Satan, he effectively was supporting Jesus. Let us beware of criticising others of the Lord's people who may not be part of our particular fellowship, but are opposing Satan and are operating in the name of Jesus, which implies acting according to the Bible. Another lesson for the disciples and for us to learn!

Nothing is more terrible than hell (verses 42-50)

I would urge every reader to read verses 42-50 for themselves, carefully and prayerfully. The message is a most solemn one: don't let anybody allow anything to so influence us now that we end up in hell in the future. In the picture in these verses, it must be terrible to lose a hand or a foot or an eye; but nothing is more terrible than hell, where those there live for ever and the fire is not quenched (verse 48). Jesus as the faithful Servant preached the message of God faithfully and often spoke of hell. Any faithful preacher now has to speak of the reality of hell for those who do not know Jesus as their personal Saviour and Lord. At the same time it is a joy to be able to tell of heaven where Jesus now is and to where all believers in Him will go.

Mark 9 covers a lot of ground. It *opens with a view of the glory of Jesus*, which will be displayed in this world in the future. This left such an impression on the three disciples. It is amazing that Jesus asked His Father (John 17:24) that all who believe on Him should

> "be with me where I am; that they may behold my glory".

The chapter *closes with a graphic view of hell*, the absolute opposite to that opening view of glory. I wonder where your future lies.

Joseph in his own home

SERIES: LESSONS ON THE LIFE OF JOSEPH

BROADCAST DATE: 9TH AUGUST 2009

There are quite a number of Josephs in the Bible. The Joseph we will be looking at is the Joseph whose life is set out in the book of Genesis – the Joseph who is perhaps best known for receiving a coat of many colours from his father.

There usually are many ways in which the life of a Bible character can be considered. The divisions of Joseph's life can be based on his four main residencies:

1. In his own home, in the early part of his life;
2. As a slave in Potiphar's house, in Egypt;
3. In prison;
4. In King Pharaoh's palace.

In each of these residences we can consider lessons on the way in which a follower of God should live and also ways in which Joseph can be viewed as a *type*, or picture, of Christ.

Here our subject is "Joseph in his own home" and we'll divide it under six headings:

Genesis 30:22-24 Joseph's origins;

Genesis 37:2-4   Father, son and brothers;

Genesis 37:5-11   The two dreams;

Genesis 37:12-24 Sent to his brothers;

Genesis 37:25-28 Sold as a slave;

Genesis 37:29-35 The blood-stained coat.

JOSEPH'S ORIGINS (GENESIS 30:22-24)

Let's read Genesis 30:22-24:

> "And God remembered Rachel, and God hear-
> kened to her, and opened her womb. And she
> conceived, and bare a son; and said, God hath
> taken away my reproach: and she called his name
> Joseph; and said, The LORD shall add to me
> another son."

Joseph's father was Jacob, also called Israel in the Bible. Jacob had two wives, both sisters. The older one, Leah, had borne him a number of sons. Now Rachel's prayers were answered and Joseph was her firstborn son, Jacob's eleventh son. Joseph's name means 'He shall add' and Rachel's prayer was answered in that later God did add a second son, Benjamin, to her.

In looking at Bible types, we must always take care not to push all the details to try to unearth parallels. However, in noting some ways in which Joseph is a type of Christ I wonder if we start to see some pointers in these early verses. Both Joseph and Jesus were the *first-born sons* of their respective mothers. If Joseph means 'He shall add', the New Testament teaches us that *in Christ many shall be made sons* (Hebrews 2:10), effectively God adding to the new line established by Jesus in His death and resurrection.

FATHER, SON AND BROTHERS (GENESIS 37:2-4)

For the rest of our considerations, we turn to Genesis 37. In looking at our second heading, let's read verses 2-4:

> "These are the generations of Jacob. Joseph, being seventeen years old, was feeding the flock with his brethren; and the lad was with the sons of Bilhah, and with the sons of Zilpah, his father's wives: and Joseph brought unto his father their evil report. Now Israel loved Joseph more than all his children, because he was the son of his old age: and he made him a coat of many colours. And when his brethren saw that their father loved him more than all his brethren, they hated him, and could not speak peaceably unto him."

We don't read anything about Joseph between his birth and this chapter, when he is 17 years old. Here is another example of a future servant of God being trained as a shepherd. I wasn't brought up on a farm but in my teenage years I spent many a happy holiday with kind Christian farming families in Northumberland. All of the farmers were shepherds and I saw for myself their dedication, patience and very hard work. What amazed me as much as anything was their knowledge of the sheep. These shepherds were not so much looking after a flock of sheep, they were caring for a large number of individual sheep, each with its own tendencies. What a good training ground for learning to care for human sheep! Simon Peter was told by Jesus to shepherd and tend the sheep and lambs. Today, our churches need dedicated, hardworking, caring men and women who really do have a heartfelt love for their fellow believers, young and old, and who seek to guide and feed those believers in God's things, recognising the differing needs of individuals. Joseph had a grounding in caring for the sheep.

The verses which we have just read tell us that Joseph was the favourite son of his father, Jacob. Jacob himself had been brought up in a home divided by favouritism and jealousy. Jacob was the favourite son of his scheming mother, Rebekah, while his brother, Esau, was favoured by his father. Now Jacob is repeating the mistake and is dividing his own home in Canaan. He favoured one wife over the other and now shows favouritism for one out of his twelve sons.

I am pleased that I have never had a home divided by favouritism. My wife and I have two grown up children whom we love equally strongly. Surely we don't need to stress the hurt which favouritism in our homes can generate. But let me extend this principle to our churches, which are our spiritual homes. How easy it is there to show partiality. The Bible would teach us to love all our fellow believers equally and failure to do this can result in the discord which we see in the home in which Joseph was brought up.

That must have been an unhappy home. Even when caring for the sheep, it would seem from verse 2 that some of Joseph's brothers caused him problems which Joseph reported back to his father. When Jacob exacerbated things by presenting Joseph with the coat of many colours, verse 4 tells us that his brothers actually hated him and could not speak in a friendly way to him. This was inevitable because the coat presented by his father would make Joseph stand out from his brothers.

What do we see of Joseph being a picture of Christ in these three verses? We don't need to have a detailed knowledge of the New Testament to know of *the great love which God the Father has for His Son,* Jesus. As Joseph's coat distinguished him from his brothers, so *God the Father ensures that everybody realises that His Son, Jesus, is unique.* For example, at the time of the transfiguration recorded in Matthew 17:1-9, when Peter equated Moses and Elijah with Jesus, God spoke from heaven and said (ve rse 5):

> "This is my beloved Son, in whom I am well pleased; hear ye him."

Joseph's coat must have been an array of beautiful colours. No doubt Joseph would sometimes wear the coat and sometimes not. In His life in this world as recorded in the four Gospels, *Jesus displayed a marvellous array of beauties and qualities.* The difference is that Jesus didn't put those beauties and qualities on and off; *those things were an integral part of Himself!*

Sadly, we must also take note that, just as Joseph was hated by his brothers, so *Jesus was hated by His own people.* Let me support this by two quotations from John's Gospel. In 1:11 it says that:

> "He came unto his own, and his own received him not."

In 15:25 it is recorded that:

> "They hated me without a cause."

Look at the scenes surrounding the cross of Jesus to note the extent of the hatred of the Jews against Him.

THE TWO DREAMS (GENESIS 37:5-11)

We move on now to our third heading, the two dreams. In the first dream, Joseph saw a harvest scene. All the brothers were binding sheaves of corn and the brothers' sheaves all bowed down to Joseph's sheaf. Rather unwisely, Joseph told this dream in all its detail to his brothers. Not surprisingly, his brothers strongly rejected the suggestion that they would ever bow down to Joseph and verse 8 tells us that they hated Joseph even more because of his dreams and what he had said.

Joseph then dreamed a second dream. This time the setting is in the sky and the sun, moon and eleven stars bowed down to Joseph. He relayed this dream to his brothers and then to his father and brothers. Jacob rebuked Joseph and questioned whether Jacob, Rachel and Joseph's brothers would ever have cause to bow down to Joseph. The result was that Joseph's brothers envied him, although Jacob pondered over what had been said.

At this stage, no member of Jacob's family could have envisaged making homage to the second youngest member of the family. However, God can see the end from the beginning and eventually the time came when all members of his family did indeed bow the knee to Joseph.

These dreams of Joseph were not ordinary dreams. There are a number of further dreams to come in the story of Joseph and God was speaking in those dreams to foretell events. There was never any doubt that those events would take place, but God would choose His timing and Joseph and others would have to wait on that timing. We don't ever read of Joseph showing impatience or urging God to move things on; he waited for God's timing, which is always perfect.

We are privileged today to have God's Word, the Bible, available to us at all times. In it, God tells us of events to take place in the future. It is not for us to know when these events will occur, but occur they certainly will, in God's timing. For example, the New Testament teaches that Jesus is coming back to take all Christians alive at that time out of this world to be with Himself and to join with all Christians who previously have died. This is sometimes referred to as *the Rapture.* When the Rapture will occur, we don't know, because the Bible explicitly says that only God knows the timing. The Rapture will certainly take place, because the Bible says so, and it is not for us to question God's timing, even though Christians long to see Jesus.

On a practical level, sometimes God makes it clear to an individual Christian that certain things will occur affecting that Christian's life, just as Joseph's dreams envisaged future events affecting him. Again, the timing of such events is in God's hands and it is necessary to await that timing with patience, never questioning.

In this section, we can see another parallel with what happened to Jesus. Verse 11 of our chapter tells us that Joseph's brothers were *envious of him.* When Pilate, the Roman governor, was judging Jesus ahead of the crucifixion, it says in Matthew 27:18:

> "For he (Pilate) knew that for envy they (the Jews) had delivered him (Jesus)."

SENT TO HIS BROTHERS (GENESIS 37:12-24)

Now to our fourth heading. Let's start by reading verses 12-13:

> "And his brethren went to feed their father's flock in Shechem. And Israel said unto Joseph, Do not thy brethren feed the flock in Shechem? come, and I will send thee unto them. And he said to him, Here am I."

First of all, notice Joseph's obedience to his father. Naturally speaking, Joseph may have had reservations about this particular instruction from Jacob. But Joseph displays no disagreement or hesitation. Immediately he makes himself fully available for the task. Today, God is looking for believers to serve Him, not necessarily in dramatic tasks, perhaps just in what seem fairly ordinary things such as was the case in this job required of Joseph. Do I obey God's voice fully and readily, when called? This task required of Joseph led to a long and difficult series of events but eventually great blessing resulted. God expects us to be obedient to His instructions and that lays the basis for God to bless in the way and at the time He chooses.

Of course, the supreme example of *perfect obedience to God* was found in Jesus. Using Joseph's words in verse 13, Jesus said: "Here am I" when God looked for someone to do the work of salvation. Taking further words from Hebrews 10:9, Jesus said:

"Lo, I come to do thy will, O God."

The perfect obedience of Jesus in going to Calvary to die for sin enabled God to come out in great blessing to mankind.

Returning to Genesis 37:12-24, as Joseph journeyed a man found him wandering in a field and asked him what he was seeking. Joseph replied (verse 16):

"I seek my brethren".

Again, I feel that we can apply this to the Lord Jesus who came from heaven *seeking those who would become His own*, those who were bought by Him at the cost of His blood shed on the cross. Prophetically, Psalm 22:22 looks forward to this when it says:

"I will declare thy name unto my brethren".

Joseph continues his journey and his brothers recognise him from a distance. Far from being pleased to see him, his brothers plot to kill him. Reuben, the oldest brother, persuades them not to kill Joseph directly but to put him into a pit, having stripped him of the coat of many colours. Later on in 42:21, we learn that Joseph pleaded from the pit for them to release him, but they ignored his pleas.

There are remarkable parallels here with what happened to Jesus. Near the end of Matthew 21, Jesus tells a parable about a man who planted a vineyard and rented it out, with the man reserving the right to receive some of the fruit. At the time the fruit was ready, the man sent his servants to collect his share but those who rented the vineyard killed the servants. This happened a second time. The man then sent his son, thinking that they would respect him. In verse 38 of that chapter it records the men as saying:

"This is the heir; come, let us kill him..."

That parable depicted God initially sending various prophets and finally His Son, Jesus, whom men killed at the cross. How similar to what happened to Joseph.

As mentioned, Joseph's *cries for help were ignored*. In Psalm 69:20, looking forward to Jesus at the cross, it says:

"I looked for some to take pity, but there was none; and for comforters, but I found none."

Sold as a slave (Genesis 37:25-28)

Now to the fifth section of this message, covering Genesis 37:25-28:

"And they (Joseph's brothers) sat down to eat bread: and they lifted up their eyes and looked, and, behold, a company of Ishmeelites came from Gilead with their camels bearing spicery and balm and myrrh, going to carry it down to Egypt. And Judah said unto his brethren, What profit is it if we slay our brother, and conceal his blood? Come, and let us sell him to the Ishmeelites, and let not our hand be upon him; for he is our brother and our flesh. And his brethren were content. Then there passed by Midianites merchantmen; and they drew and lifted up Joseph out of the pit, and sold Joseph to the Ishmeelites for twenty pieces of silver: and they brought Joseph into Egypt."

I wonder what Joseph thought at this stage. How did being sold as a slave fit with the dreams where his family bowed down to him? Whatever his thoughts, we don't read of Joseph ever questioning God's plan, either here or in the difficult circumstances which occurred later. There is a lesson here for all Christians that, whatever the severity of the short term problems may be, God's ultimate plan for us will not be thwarted and will come to pass. In all Joseph's difficulties, God remained close to him.

Once again in this section we see some remarkable similarities to the experiences of the Lord Jesus. In a general sense, we can see Joseph's path descending from his favoured position in his father's house to the pit and then to being sold as a slave and going into Egypt. We can see further downward steps in chapters 39 and 40, before Joseph is exalted in chapter 41. If you have time, read Philippians 2:6-8 where the *downward steps* of Christ Jesus are recorded, from His position with His Father in heaven right down to the death of the cross. Philippians 2:9-11 then record the *exaltation* of Jesus.

In this fifth section we see that Judah, one of Joseph's brothers, suggested making money out of getting rid of Joseph, who was then sold to the passing merchantmen for 20 pieces of silver. We immediately think of Judas Iscariot, one of the 12 disciples and therefore *close* to Jesus, as Judah was close to Joseph. Judas betrayed Jesus and *sold Him* for 30 pieces of silver, making money out of getting rid of Jesus. Even in that terrible betrayal, the accuracy of Scripture is touching to note, because the Bible says (Colossians 1:18):

> "… that in all things he (Christ) might have the preeminence."

Joseph was sold for 20 pieces of silver but Jesus for 30!

THE BLOOD-STAINED COAT (GENESIS 37:29-35)

So, Joseph is brought into Egypt by the merchantmen. However, Genesis 37 is not quite finished.

Joseph's brothers faced a dilemma. As far as they were concerned, they had got rid of Joseph, although years later they would see that this was not the case. However, they did not want to admit to their father that they both instigated and implemented the plan for the disappearance of their father's favourite son. Accordingly, they killed a young goat, dipped Joseph's coat of many colours in the goat's blood and brought the blood-stained coat to Jacob with the lie that they had found the coat.

Jacob was distraught when presented with this lie. Naturally he assumed that a wild beast had killed Joseph. Jacob tore his clothes, mourned many days and refused to be comforted.

Often, sin is like a treadmill. To try to cover up the first sin, further sins are committed. How often telling lies is a part of that sinful process. God's Word is quite clear, including the ninth of the Ten Commandments, that to lie is a sin, and all sins are against God. The Bible never talks about white lies or little lies. We never read of Joseph telling a lie, even when others lied about him. *Jesus was the embodiment of truth*, the opposite to our enemy, Satan, who is described as the father of lies (John 8:44). As Christians, we should be known as those, like Jesus, who always speak the absolute truth, even if in the short term it proves costly.

Another matter to note from this final section is that when sin takes place, its effects often extend beyond those committing the sin to cause problems to others. Joseph's brothers sinned and the result was that their father was broken-hearted with sorrow. Verse 35 of our chapter contains Jacob's words:

> "For I will go down into the grave unto my son mourning. Thus his father wept for him."

Sin is a dreadful thing and causes misery and distress. We only need to read any daily newspaper to see that.

Joseph is one of those Bible characters like Joshua, Caleb and Daniel where very little of criticism is noted in the Bible. I trust that we can learn from Joseph's way of life as a follower of God. I trust also that we can gain an even greater appreciation of Christ by seeing the parallels contained in the Old Testament but shown in much greater wonder when Jesus is revealed in the New Testament.

Choosing to follow God – Ruth 1

SERIES: CHOICES (FROM THE BOOK OF RUTH)

BROADCAST DATE: 18TH OCTOBER 2009

There are only two books in the Bible which carry the names of women. Both are in the Old Testament. Both paint pictures of women who have attractive, loyal and determined characters. The first of these women is Ruth and the second, Esther.

The book of Ruth is a short book with only four chapters, which we can summarise with the headings:

Ruth 1	Choosing to follow God;
Ruth 2	Choosing to serve God;
Ruth 3	Choosing a wife;
Ruth 4	Choosing to do things the right way.

As the first verse of the book tells us, the events of Ruth are set in the times when the judges ruled Israel, that is the times described in the Bible book prior to Ruth, the book of Judges. Exactly when in the times of the judges Ruth lived we are not told. However, most of those times were bleak. God's people, Israel, kept forsaking Him and God brought punishments on them via the surrounding tribes. When Israel could not bear the punishment, they prayed to God for help. God then provided a judge who delivered them. For a while, Israel would then be faithful to God but soon would return to their old ways. The whole pattern was then repeated. The last verse of Judges reads:

> "In those days there was no king in Israel: every man did that which was right in his own eyes" (Judges 21:25).

Immediately after that verse appears the delightful little book of Ruth which, although beginning with failure, ends with the mention of David, the king through whose line Christ would appear. In the Bible, eight often speaks of a new beginning. Ruth is the eighth book in the Bible, introducing hints of a new beginning through Christ, after the failure of what occurred before He came into the world.

I thank God for those dear Christians who in my younger days built up my appreciation of the Old Testament and showed me some of the *types*, or pictures, of future events which can be drawn from these early Bible books. In looking at Ruth, I want to suggest just some of those pictures.

So, we turn to our subject: chapter 1 of Ruth, with the title "Choosing to follow God". I would like to divide this chapter into four sections:

verses 1-5	Going to Moab;
verses 6-7	Leaving Moab;
verses 8-18	Decision time;
verses 19-22	Back in Bethlehem.

GOING TO MOAB (VERSES 1-5)

We begin this first section with verses 1-5:

> "Now it came to pass in the days when the judges ruled, that there was a famine in the land. And a certain man of Bethlehem-judah went to sojourn in the country of Moab, he, and his wife, and his two sons. And the name of the man was Elimelech, and the name of his wife Naomi, and the name of his two sons Mahlon and Chilion, Ephrathites of Bethlehem-judah. And they came into the country of Moab, and continued there. And Elimelech Naomi's husband died; and she was left, and her two sons. And they took them wives of the women of Moab: the name of the one was Orpah, and the name of the other Ruth: and they dwelt there about ten years. And Mahlon and Chilion died also both of them; and the woman was left of her two sons and her husband."

In these verses we are introduced to six of the seven named characters in the actions in the book of Ruth; the seventh is Boaz, who is brought in at the very first verse of chapter 2. The first four characters are Elimelech, his wife Naomi and their two sons, Mahlon and Chilion. Elimelech, as head of his family, was faced with a difficult situation. His home town, Bethlehem, was suffering from a severe famine. Should he move from his home in the land of promise given to Elimelech's people by God? Elimelech decides to move his family to Moab where there is food. In Moab, Elimelech dies. His two sons marry girls from Moab, Mahlon marrying Ruth and Chilion marrying Orpah. Then Mahlon and Chilion die. Naomi had lost the three men in her life. She, Ruth and Orpah were all widows.

In Bible times, the meaning of names is important. Parents named their children bearing in mind the meaning of the name given. Look at the instances when God changed someone's name; there was always a reason for the change as God wanted to convey something by the meaning of the new name. Place names also had important meanings. *Bethlehem* means 'house of bread', yet here was a situation where there was no food in the house of bread! Was God trying to tell Elimelech something? We don't read of Elimelech praying about this matter, seeking God's mind. On the face of it, the decision he took to move his family seems perfectly reasonable; his main concern surely was to ensure the physical wellbeing of his sons and wife. But for a follower of God is that really the matter of over-riding importance? The Bible teaches us that our spiritual needs come first; in 1 Thessalonians 5:23 the divine order is spirit, soul and body and not, as often misquoted, body, soul and spirit. Where did God's things fit into Elimelech's reckoning? The people of Moab had regularly been Israel's enemies and they worshipped false gods. Living amongst them might get food in the short term but at what cost to the spiritual wellbeing of his wife and sons?

Elimelech's name means 'to whom God is king'. Elimelech is one of those people whose actions did not live up to his name. He didn't make God king of his life. The consequences of his decision to move to Moab were disastrous for his family. He died leaving them in a strange land with no head of the family, his sons married girls who were not followers of the true God and then his sons both died.

Here are lessons for Christians today. How important it is always to put God's things first, to pray long and hard about matters until God makes His mind clear to us. Dear reader, I'm not suggesting it was easy for Elimelech; it was a hugely difficult decision for him and ensuring that the spiritual welfare of our families comes before everything else is no easy thing for us. Elimelech shouldn't have left God's house of bread whatever the short term difficulties might have seemed and whatever the superficial attractions of Moab appeared to be. Moab was a spiritually dangerous place.

LEAVING MOAB (VERSES 6-7)

In the second section of our chapter, Naomi, Elimelech's widow, hears that there is food again back in Bethlehem. Presumably there continued to be food available in Moab. But after more than ten years in Moab Naomi is faced with a decision: will she choose the bread of Bethlehem, God's place, or the bread of Moab, the world?

Let us think a little more about Naomi. Her name means 'pleasant' and, despite all her problems, she comes across as an impressive woman, devoted to her family. Whatever she thought of her husband's decision to move from Bethlehem to Moab, she remained loyal to him. We will see shortly that, in Moab, she must have shown a testimony to God sufficient to introduce God to her daughter in law, Ruth. Through chapters 2, 3, and 4 Naomi provides sound advice to Ruth and is always there to give support. What an invaluable role a godly woman can have! She lives up to her name by having a pleasant and wholesome effect on others.

In verses 6-7, Naomi makes the right decision. She puts aside the bread of Moab and sets out to return to the bread in the place provided by God. Today, Christians can't be sustained and built up other than by feeding on

Jesus, who said, "I am the bread of life", and on the Word of God, the Bible. Naomi would have got nowhere spiritually if she had remained in Moab. She set out to return, taking her daughters in law with her. If any Christian has strayed from God's things, a return in repentance is always possible, but that initial decision to return and then real action to return must come from the individual.

DECISION TIME (VERSES 8-18)

We come now to the third section of our chapter. Let's start by reading from verse 8 to the beginning of verse 11:.

> "And Naomi said unto her two daughters in law, Go, return each to her mother's house: the LORD deal kindly with you, as ye have dealt with the dead, and with me. The LORD grant you that ye may find rest, each of you in the house of her husband. Then she kissed them; and they lifted up their voice, and wept. And they said unto her, Surely we will return with thee unto thy people. And Naomi said, Turn again, my daughters: why will ye go with me?"

Naomi then goes on to tell her daughters in law that there are no natural reasons why they should go with her. Naomi says that she is too old to have another husband and to bear sons. Even if she did, her daughters in law would not wait until those sons became old enough to marry. She urged them to go back to their people.

Why did Naomi go out of her way to emphasise to her daughters in law all the downsides if they were to go with her to Bethlehem? Surely it could only be a good thing for these two young ladies to move from Moab, a land of idol worship, to Israel where the true God was known. And yet Naomi seems almost to discourage them from going with her.

Could the Bible here be presenting an important principle? Clearly, Naomi had maintained a testimony to God in her home; the evidence for that is in verses 16-17 of our chapter, which we will come to shortly when we consider Ruth's response to Naomi. But these young ladies each had to make up their own minds, not to be committed to Naomi, but to be committed to Naomi's God. They would be stepping out into an uncertain future with no possessions in a country strange to them. Things would be much easier with support back home from their families. Naomi could help and guide but unless Ruth and Orpah each had a personal commitment to God, the way ahead might prove difficult. It is no different today. The Christian life is tremendous and has a promised goal of being in heaven with Jesus for eternity. But that life is not easy and unless it is underpinned by a firm personal relationship with the Lord Jesus, problems will arise.

We now pick up the Bible narrative for this third section, from verse 14:

> "And they lifted up their voice, and wept again: and Orpah kissed her mother in law; but Ruth clave unto her. And she said, Behold, thy sister in law is gone back unto her people, and unto her gods: return thou after thy sister in law. And Ruth said, Intreat me not to leave thee, or to return from following after thee: for whither thou goest, I will go; and where thou lodgest, I will lodge: thy people shall be my people, and thy God my God: where thou diest, will I die, and there will I be buried: the LORD do so to me, and more also, if

ought but death part thee and me. When she saw that she was stedfastly minded to go with her, then she left speaking unto her."

In these verses 14-18, we have the differing responses of the two young ladies to what their mother in law had presented to them. Each of them had to make up her own mind. This is why our chapter has the title "Choosing to follow God". Orpah was full of tears and kissed Naomi. Orpah chose to go back to her own people and, following the application which we are giving this true story, turned her back on God, not prepared to step out for Him. We don't read any more about Orpah.

What a lovely contrast there is in the choice made by Ruth! She wasn't deterred by her sister in law's decision, but made the choice firmly and beautifully set out in the words which we have just read in verses 16-17. Ruth chose to move to a new country, a new home, a true God, a different future. There was the expression of full commitment to God. It effectively is what we would nowadays call confessing Jesus as Lord, not just acknowledging Him as Saviour. Here near the border of Moab and Israel is a young woman facing lots of uncertainties but sure in her knowledge that she is committing herself to the Lordship of heaven. It fits perfectly with what Paul and Silas told the jailor in Philippi:

"Believe on the Lord Jesus Christ, and thou shalt be saved" (Acts 16:31)

and with what Paul wrote in Romans 10:9:

"That if thou shalt confess with thy mouth the Lord Jesus (that is, Jesus as Lord), and shalt believe in thine heart that God hath raised him from the dead, thou shalt be saved."

When anyone becomes a Christian, that person is moving from the control of one master, Satan, to be subject to the control of a new Master, the Lord Jesus Christ. The Lord's control is demanding but not onerous. A Christian is expected, not to live for himself or herself, but to live for the One, as Galatians 2:20 says,

"who loved me, and gave himself for me."

In this Old Testament picture, Ruth made this commitment in these verses. We never read of her practically falling short of that statement. I find this quite a challenge.

Last year, my wife and I had the privilege of being present at a Christian wedding in Bristol. Verses 16-17 of our chapter were used in the wedding service as a statement of commitment between bridegroom and bride. I had never heard that before in a wedding service but Scriptures often can be applied in a number of ways. Commitment to one another in marriage vows is important. Real commitment to the Lord Jesus is vital for Christians. Ruth has much to teach us.

When Naomi perceived that Ruth had made up her mind to continue with her to Bethlehem, Naomi accepted the situation, no doubt happy for Ruth to be with her. A good thing to be "stedfastly minded" to proceed along the way ahead, just like Ruth in verse 18.

BACK TO BETHLEHEM (VERSES 19-22)

This brings us to the final section of Ruth 1. Let's read verses 19-21:

"So they two went until they came to Bethlehem. And it came to pass, when they were come to Bethlehem, that all the city was moved about them, and they said, Is this Naomi? And she said unto them, Call me not Naomi, call me Mara: for the Almighty hath dealt very bitterly with me. I went out full, and the LORD hath brought me home again empty: why then call ye me Naomi, seeing the LORD hath testified against me, and the Almighty hath afflicted me?"

It had been many years since Naomi had left Bethlehem with her husband and two sons. The years away had been tragic ones and I don't doubt that not only would Naomi have aged in the natural process of growing older, but also the sorrow of sad events would have left their mark. As we noted earlier, Naomi's name means 'pleasant' but she suggests to the Bethlehem women that it would now be more appropriate to call her Mara, which means 'bitter'. In leading her to come back to her spiritual home, God had had to take her through many difficult circumstances so that she was now empty of all that she possessed when she left Bethlehem. Sometimes when we as Christians stray from our spiritual roots, God has to take us through difficult circumstances to show us that our true resources are only in Him and where He directs. God always aims for restoration and blessing for His people. At this stage, Naomi did not know that blessing would come through Ruth.

The last verse of chapter 1 reads as follows:

"So Naomi returned, and Ruth the Moabitess, her daughter in law, with her, which returned out of the country of Moab: and they came to Bethlehem in the beginning of barley harvest."

In this last verse, I would like to draw attention to the phrase "Ruth the Moabitess". This is the first of five times in the book of Ruth that this phrase is used. Let us spend a short time considering what it meant to belong to the tribe and land of Moab. If you were to read the last few verses of Genesis 19, you would see that Abraham's nephew, Lot, became drunk on consecutive nights and his two daughters slept with him. They both became pregnant. The sons born as a result of these sad events were called Moab and Benammi and their descendants, the Moabites and the Ammonites, became enemies of God's people, the Children of Israel. The tribe of Moab settled on the east side of the Dead Sea. The Old Testament has many prophecies against Moab. The tribe which was begun in the act of sin in Genesis 19 was excluded from God's things. For example, part of Deuteronomy 23:3 says that a

> "Moabite shall not enter into the congregation of the LORD".

In Ruth 1:22, we have the statement that

> "Ruth the Moabitess … came to Bethlehem",

the very place where around 1,300 years later Jesus would be born. As we read through the book of Ruth, we see Ruth brought more and more into God's blessing, despite being from Moab. Ruth didn't deserve it, but through Naomi's testimony and the actions of Boaz she is found by the end of the book bearing a son who was the forefather of David, in whose royal line Christ was born. Ruth is even mentioned in the genealogy of Jesus, in Matthew 1:5. Yet constantly in this book there are reminders that she was a Moabitess. What a picture of everyone who becomes a born again believer in Jesus! No believer deserves it! Each believer has been brought, like Ruth, from the distance of sin right into the presence of God the Father. What a good thing constantly to remind myself that I was like a Moabite, a sinner, and to recognise God's grace in making me one of His people.

In chapter 2, we are introduced to Boaz, the man of strength who made all the difference to Ruth. Dear reader, do you know the Lord Jesus Christ who has made all the difference to me and can change your life and destiny if you trust in Him?

Ruth's name means 'friendship'. We see this evidenced in the last verse of chapter 1 when Naomi and Ruth arrive together in Bethlehem and then in subsequent chapters where Ruth is loyal to her mother in law.

I have concentrated on a limited number of applications of the individuals in the book of Ruth. There are additional applications which can be made, particularly in seeing some of these people as being types which fit the Bible prophecies about the Jewish nation and in seeing Ruth as representing the bride of Christ.

I trust that, as you read the whole of the book of Ruth for yourself, you enjoy the relevancies and the challenges which she and other characters can bring to our Christian position and lives today. Above all, I hope that you will see the crucial influence of Boaz, pointing forward to the fact that everything that Christians have now is based on who Jesus is and what He has done.

Elijah – the champion of God – 1 Kings 18

SERIES: LESSONS FROM THE LIFE OF ELIJAH

BROADCAST DATE: 10TH JANUARY 2010

There are many lessons from the life of Elijah, which can be taken from the Old Testament book of 1 Kings. Our subject formed part of a series which looked at:

1 Kings 17:1-7	The prophet of God;
1 Kings 17:8-24	The man of God;
1 Kings 18	The champion of God;
1 Kings 19	Cast upon God.

The prophet of God

In 1 Kings 17:1-7, Elijah comes, apparently from nowhere, to confront the wicked King Ahab and to convey the message of God's judgement; there were to be years of drought which would come to an end at a time decided by God. Elijah was then instructed by God to go and hide by the brook Cherith and God commanded the ravens to take food to him. Lessons can be drawn here from Elijah's *fearlessness* in taking God's message to

Ahab, his *obedience* to God's instructions and his *dependence* on God for protection and provision.

The man of God

In 1 Kings 17:8-24, we read about Elijah being sent by God from Cherith to a place called Zarephath. There he met a widow woman who was coming to the end of the food that she had for her son and herself. God made that woman's remaining food miraculously not run out. Later the woman's son died and God used Elijah to bring him back to life again. The woman acknowledged that Elijah was *a man of God*.

The champion of God

Our subject covers the events recorded in chapter 18. If I was asked to provide my personal list of a half dozen thrilling events in the Old Testament, Elijah versus Ahab and the prophets of Baal in 1 Kings 18 would be in that list. This is not a dry, academic story but a dramatic unfolding of God's power over people and events. It is my prayer that we are left with a heart-stirring impression of Elijah's faithfulness in apparently impossible circumstances and of the unlimited power of God.

Our title is 'Elijah – the champion of God'. We will divide 1 Kings 18 into three sections:

verses 1-21	His stand for God;
verses 22-40	His confidence in God;
verses 41-46	His expectation from God.

HIS STAND FOR GOD (VERSES 1-21)

Let's start by reading 1 Kings 18:1-2:

> "And it came to pass after many days, that the word of the LORD came to Elijah in the third year, saying, Go, shew thyself unto Ahab; and I will send rain upon the earth. And Elijah went to shew

himself unto Ahab. And there was a sore famine in Samaria."

It was over three years earlier that Elijah had last seen King Ahab, when Elijah told him of God's judgement by way of a drought (see 17:1). Now God had decided that the drought would come to an end and He would make it clear that He was instigating the renewal of rainfall. The Scriptures show that Ahab was not a kind or forgiving person and yet here God was instructing Elijah personally to deliver a message to the powerful Ahab in whom three years of resentment will have built up. Instead of showing any hesitancy, Elijah immediately obeys God and sets out to find Ahab. Any believer wanting to stand for God must show obedience to what God says. Today, we have the Bible, as God's instructions to us, and every Christian should obey what God says in the Bible. We may not be called to be involved in dramatic events like Elijah in the book of Kings, but we should adhere to Bible instructions.

In verses 3-16 of our chapter we meet a man called Obadiah who was the governor of King Ahab's palace. Verse 3 tells us that "Obadiah feared the LORD greatly". There is no doubt that Obadiah was a follower of God but in my view he is an example of some who misguidedly think that they can still serve God while being linked to the world. There is a helpful note in my Schofield Reference Bible which says: "Obadiah is a warning type of the men of God who adhere to the world while still seeking to serve God. The secret of the Lord, and the power of the Lord were with Elijah, the separated servant."

Verses 5-6 tell us that at this time of famine and suffering for his people, Ahab's priority was to find grass for his horses. In the Old Testament we often find that times of famine were sent by God as a judgement for sin and unfaithfulness to Him. That was the case at the time we are considering and yet there is no indication at all that Ahab was reflecting on the likely reason for this famine. His horses were more important to him than God!

Ahab and Obadiah were searching the land to find grass for the horses. Elijah met Obadiah and told him to tell Ahab that Elijah wanted to see him. Obadiah was not keen to carry that message fearing that Ahab would kill the messenger who brought the news of the where-abouts of Elijah, for whom Ahab had spent three years unsuccessfully searching. Of course, during that time God had been protecting Elijah, as He does all His servants, and God did not allow Ahab to find Elijah until God permitted it.

Obadiah eventually agreed to relay the message and Ahab went to meet Elijah. Let's read verses 17-18:

> "And it came to pass, when Ahab saw Elijah, that Ahab said unto him, Art thou he that troubleth Israel? And he answered, I have not troubled Israel; but thou, and thy father's house, in that ye have forsaken the commandments of the LORD, and thou hast followed Baalim."

I should add here that Baal was the chief male god of the heathen Canaanites.

What a straight statement by Elijah! He showed no fear in stating God's message to the powerful king and he did not shirk from pointing to Ahab's personal responsibility for disobeying God's word and for following false gods. No mistaking this message! Would that Christians always made God's message "clear and plain", as one old hymn writer once put it.

Elijah then told Ahab to instruct all the people of Israel and the 450 prophets of the false god Baal, to congregate at Mount Carmel, which is near the Mediterranean coast. Elijah addressed the congregation with these words, recorded in verse 21:

> "How long halt ye between two opinions? If the LORD be God, follow him: but if Baal, then follow him."

The verse ends with the statement:

> "And the people answered him not a word."

Elijah made his stand for God at Mount Carmel in front of Ahab, the prophets of the false god Baal and all the people. Elijah knew the power, the holiness, the faithfulness of the true God, his God, and he did not hesitate to speak out in front of this huge audience. Elijah gave them a choice, either to follow the true God who had been faithful to Israel over hundreds of years or to follow the false god, Baal. The people would not choose God. In the presence of evil, idolatry and unfaithfulness, Elijah stood for God. In this our time and in our country, we need to take a similar stand.

HIS CONFIDENCE IN GOD (VERSES *22-40*)

This brings us to the second section of our chapter. The people had not responded to Elijah's demand that they choose between God and Baal. Elijah now issues them with a challenge, which is contained in verses 22-24:

> "Then said Elijah unto the people, I, even I only, remain a prophet of the LORD; but Baal's prophets are four hundred and fifty men. Let them there-

fore give us two bullocks; and let them choose one bullock for themselves, and cut it in pieces, and lay it on wood, and put no fire under: and I will dress the other bullock, and lay it on wood, and put no fire under: and call ye on the name of your gods, and I will call on the name of the LORD: and the God that answereth by fire, let him be God. And all the people answered and said, It is well spoken."

So Elijah was standing alone against 450 prophets of Baal in a contest to see whether God or Baal could bring fire down to burn up a bullock. Impossible, we would say. But then, the contest was not really between Elijah and the 450. It was between God and Baal. Elijah's name means 'my God is Jehovah'. Elijah had complete confidence in his God, Jehovah the Eternal One. In this extreme circumstance, alone in front of so many people, Elijah's confidence in his God never wavered. I ask myself, does my confidence in God ever waver? Do I ever doubt the absolute promises of God contained in the Bible, such as Romans 8:28:

"All things work together for good to them that love God",

or Philippians 4:19:

"My God shall supply all your need"?

The fact is that if God can fail then He is not God. The possibility of God failing never entered Elijah's mind. May my confidence in God always be equally strong!

And so the contest began. It lasted all day. The crowd was huge and gripped by the dramatic events on display. The 450 prophets of Baal started the contest. They chose their bullock, prepared it, placed it on the wood and started to pray to Baal to bring fire to consume the bullock. They prayed all morning without any result. At midday Elijah mocked them, as recorded in verse 27:

> "Cry aloud: for he is a god; either he is talking, or he is pursuing, or he is in a journey, or peradventure he sleepeth, and must be awaked."

In response to Elijah's taunts the 450 prophets shouted to Baal even more loudly and cut themselves with knives. This continued all afternoon but still the body of the bullock lay on the wood with no sign of fire or anything else from Baal.

Towards evening, Elijah effectively said: "You have had all day to demonstrate the power of Baal and without success. Now it is my turn to show the power of my God". The champion of God started by building an altar of 12 stones in the name of the LORD. Round the altar he dug a trench. Then he put wood on the altar and on top of the wood he placed the pieces of bullock. Next he instructed that four barrels of water be poured over the meat and the wood. Then another four barrels. And a further four barrels. Then he topped up the trench with more water. You can imagine the crowd not believing what they were seeing! All day they had watched 450 prophets of Baal pleading with Baal to send fire on the meat and wood, but with no response. Now here was Elijah soaking the wood, meat and surroundings with water, the last thing someone does when fire is wanted. Perhaps they thought Elijah was mad! He was either that or he had unlimited confidence in God.

Elijah then proceeded to pray, using these words recorded in 1 Kings 18:36-37:

> "LORD God of Abraham, Isaac, and of Israel, let it be known this day that thou art God in Israel, and

that I am thy servant, and that I have done all these things at thy word. Hear me, O LORD, hear me, that this people may know that thou art the LORD God, and that thou hast turned their heart back again."

God immediately answered that prayer from His servant. The chapter tells us that the fire of the LORD consumed the meat, the wood, the stones and dust and the water in the trench. Nothing was left! God's power and the power of faith and the power of prayer were all evidenced in dramatic fashion.

And what of the effect of all this on the watching crowd of people? They had seen 450 prophets of Baal produce no result all day, whereas one prophet of God brought a result in a short period of time. The key was the Person in whom Elijah believed. Baal was a false god with no more power or life than the pile of stones and wood. Elijah's God was alive, an all-powerful Creator God who had sustained His people ever since they left Egypt.

Whereas the people had had nothing to say when challenged earlier by Elijah to choose between God and Baal, they now twice said: "The LORD, he is the God." All of the prophets of Baal were taken and killed.

That acknowledgement of God, inferring repentance on behalf of the people, cleared the way for God to come out in blessing. Now in the next section of the chapter, reference can be made to the return of rain. It is the Old Testament pattern of God's judgement, repentance by the people and then God's blessing. And God wants to bless and not in half measures; verse 41 will tell us of "abundance of rain" and verse 45 of "great rain".

To summarise, what spiritual lessons can be taken from this second section of 1 Kings 18? I suggest that these might include:

- God's power is unlimited.
- When in a minority or even all alone, the fact that there is a large opposition does not mean that they are right or that they will win.
- When faced with evil, don't compromise on God's standards.
- Prayer to God is powerful.
- Idols can be attractive but are useless.
- God will put down all evil in His timing.
- Elijah built an altar in the name of the Lord. God's name incorporates His fame. Let us always honour His name.

HIS EXPECTATION FROM GOD (VERSES 41-46)

I would like us to read some of the verses in this final section of 1 Kings 18:

> "And Elijah said unto Ahab, Get thee up, eat and drink; for there is a sound of abundance of rain. So Ahab went up to eat and to drink. And Elijah went up to the top of Carmel; and he cast himself down upon the earth, and put his face between his knees, And said to his servant, Go up now, look towards the sea. And he went up, and looked, and said, There is nothing. And he said, Go again seven times. And it came to pass at the seventh time, that he said, Behold, there ariseth a little cloud out of the sea, like a man's hand. … And it came to pass in the mean while, that the heaven was black with clouds and wind, and there was a great rain."

From these verses, first of all consider King Ahab. Earlier in the chapter we thought about Ahab's prime concern at this time of drought and famine being finding grass for his horses. Now, having seen the dramatic display of God's power and the execution of the 450 prophets of Baal, Ahab hears Elijah talk of the promise of rain returning for the first time in 3½ years. Is there any sign of repentance by Ahab, any suggestion that he acknowledges, as the people did, that "The LORD, he is the God"? No sign at all! Despite what he has witnessed, Ahab thinks of nobody but himself and utters not one word of repentance toward God or acknowledgement of God's greatness. Ahab has no spiritual consciousness at all and therefore cannot hear God speaking.

Now compare this with Elijah! Far from relaxing after the demands on him set out in this chapter, Elijah immediately goes with his servant to spend time with God on Mount Carmel. Elijah and every servant of God needs time with God, not just before and during a time of service, but also afterwards, in commending that service to God and asking for His blessing upon it. I ask myself whether I spend as much time in God's presence after a time of service as I do before it.

Ever since Elijah so abruptly appeared on the scene in 1 Kings 17:1 he has been shown to be a man of prayer. We learn that from James 5:17 where it says that

> "Elias (Elijah) was a man subject to like passions as we are, and he prayed earnestly that it might not rain: …"

Earlier we saw that Elijah prayed for God to send down fire on the sacrifice. The verses I have read in this third section of 1 Kings 18 give details of Elijah's praying on Mount Carmel.

Alone with God

First we see that this servant of God went to be alone with God so that there could be communion between heaven and himself. Church prayers and family prayers are of great importance and value but for an individual servant of God time spent alone with God is also of great importance and value. In the Gospels we read of Jesus spending lengthy time in private prayer with His Father. What a good thing for us to tell the Lord all about our service and to seek guidance, encouragement and direction.

Humility and reverence

Then we note in verse 42 that Elijah "cast himself down upon the earth, and put his face between his knees". His approach to God was one of humility and reverence. Elijah wasn't taking any credit for the defeat of Baal. He was acknowledging that he was in the presence of the God of power who alone had wrought that recent miracle. Today, we have the great privilege, as Elijah never did, of knowing God as our Father, with all the nearness of relationship which this brings; but never let us forget as we approach Him that our Father is still God, worthy of all reverence and honour.

Persistent

Thirdly, we see that Elijah was persistent in prayer. He did not give up praying when his servant had been to the top of Carmel six times and still not seen the slightest sign of any approaching rain. Was God testing Elijah's faith in this? I don't know, but certainly Elijah did not stop praying. I find this challenging as I reflect that over the years I may not have been as persistent in prayer on particular matters as I might have been.

Spiritually minded

Lastly, I note that Elijah was so spiritually minded that he was able to detect God's full response to his prayer by the smallest sign from heaven. On his seventh visit to the top of Carmel the servant reported that "there ariseth a little cloud out of the sea, like a man's hand." All of the rest of the sky remained clear blue, but Elijah, man of God, man of faith, man of prayer, knew from this tiny cloud that God was giving a sign of His answer to prayer, a sign of great things to come. The sky was soon black with clouds and there was a great rain. The drought was over, in God's timing. God was demonstrating His control through these miraculous events.

Again, Elijah's example causes me to reflect whether I am sufficiently spiritually minded to know when God is giving me a sign, maybe through an apparently small event, that He has answered prayer and He is going to do great things in the future. Those great things may or may not come as quickly as the great rain followed on the sighting of the tiny cloud, but come they will if God is in it.

I do trust that this thrilling chapter is both a help and challenge to every believer in the Lord Jesus Christ. The power of Elijah's God, the only true God, is no less today. What a God we Christians have!

About the Author

By profession an accountant, and by calling a Christian, the passage of scripture read on 8 March 2010 at the service of thanksgiving to celebrate Glenn Baxter's life summed up both his life and ministry:

> We have our hope set on the living God, who is the Saviour of all people, especially of those who believe. Command and teach these things. Let no one despise you for your youth, but set the believers an example in speech, in conduct, in love, in faith, in purity. Until I come, devote yourself to the public reading of Scripture, to exhortation, to teaching. Do not neglect the gift you have, which was given you by prophecy when the council of elders laid their hands on you. Practice these things, immerse yourself in them, so that all may see your progress. Keep a close watch on yourself and on the teaching. Persist in this, for by so doing you will save both yourself and your hearers.

1 Timothy 4:10b-16 (ESV)

The following, from the thanksgiving address by Peter Ollerhead, reflects the deep respect and gratitude of many for Glenn's loyalty, service and example.

LOYALTY – RUTH 1:16

And Ruth said, Intreat me not to leave thee, or to return from following after thee: for whither thou goest, I will go; and where thou lodgest, I will lodge: thy people shall be my people, and thy God my God.

One thing that marked Glenn was his loyalty. I have four things on which Glenn was loyal – he made a pledge and kept to it:

1. Glenn was brought to love the Lord Jesus when he was eight years old and became *a Christian,* and he lived his life in the faith of the Lord Jesus.

2. The implication of the promise that he made when young, was that he became *a servant of God.* Glenn was serving the Lord in the Gospel – preaching at Cromwell Hall, Levenshulme, Manchester the afternoon before his stroke – he remained loyal to the service of Christ to the end.

3. Thirdly, he was loyal to was *the assembly* in Old Park Lane, Southport. He did not exclude the testimony that other Christians made, but there was something precious about the testimony from Old Park Lane when Glenn joined there, and he remained loyal to that particular expression of the Christian faith.

4. 33 years ago he and Jackie stood together at Edgefield Gospel Hall, Fawdon, Newcastle-upon-Tyne and they made a pledge to one another. Glenn was loyal to that pledge – loyal to his duties as *a husband and father.*

A SERVANT OF THE LORD – DEUTERONOMY 34:5-8

> So Moses the servant of the Lord died there in the land
> of Moab, according to the word of the Lord. And he
> buried him in a valley in the land of Moab, …: but no
> man knoweth of his sepulchre unto this day. And Moses
> was an hundred and twenty years old when he died: his
> eye was not dim, nor his natural force abated. And the
> children of Israel wept for Moses in the plains of Moab
> thirty days.

Why do I read this? Because I can change the name
there and I could say, *Glenn the servant of the LORD died
there in the land of Moab.*

… IN THE GOSPEL

A man who served the Lord Jesus whenever he was
called – wherever he was called to preach (and it was
mainly at Old Park Lane); he sought to gather many in.
He sought to preach the gospel to those and he concentrated his attention there.

One of his texts in his last Gospel preaching was John
10:11: "I am the good shepherd: the good shepherd
giveth his life for the sheep." Right to the end of his life
he wanted people to come in and to know the wonder
and the glory of the salvation of Christ – to know something of the preciousness of that Person who gave His
life for him.

… AMONGST YOUNG PEOPLE

Glenn reached, pastored and taught young people at
Southport, and beyond, in young people's meetings,
houseparties and conferences. There are many too in
the camps – the Fenham Camps – who looked to Glenn
with affection and with respect for this area of his
service.

... AT SCRIPTURE TRUTH PUBLICATIONS

The last time that I met him he was in Crewe, chairing a meeting of the trustees of STP (Scripture Truth Publications). He and David Coleman – both taken as comparatively young men – did the vast amount of work that was involved in leading STP through a change in circumstances and a change of location, from Morpeth to Crewe. He was a servant of the Lord who used his faculties in the service of Christ; not the fag-end of his life, not the little bits that he didn't want, but everything that he could muster as a family man in the service of Christ.

... WITH TRUTH FOR TODAY

For the *Truth for Today* talks that Glenn prepared, it was much more difficult for him to prepare an address than for slower speakers – he had so much he needed to say! Glenn prepared these addresses very, very carefully – as a true servant of the Lord.

AN EXAMPLE TO THE SAINTS – 2 CORINTHIANS 13:11-14

Lastly, some words in the New Testament and, if I may, I put these into the mouth of Glenn:

> Finally, brethren, farewell. Be perfect, be of good comfort, be of one mind, live in peace; and the God of love and peace shall be with you. Greet one another with an holy kiss. All the saints salute you. The grace of the Lord Jesus Christ, and the love of God, and the communion of the Holy Ghost, be with you all. Amen.

He didn't have time to say it to us all. Glenn was one that greeted you and *he was one that made sure he shook hands with you before he left.*

There is an idea amongst some that being a Christian, accepting the Lord as your Saviour, is all that is necessary; but Glenn did not stop there. He sought to bring young people into the assembly and into the full expression of Christianity, that they might become followers of Jesus. He wanted them to be *perfect*, not in the sense that they never did anything wrong, but mature in the expression of their Christian faith.

We have every right to weep for Glenn, a man deeply loved, a man deeply appreciated, a man whose presence we will miss; but we belong to the God of all *comfort* (2 Corinthians 1:3), the God of all consolation (Romans 15:5).

There's another thing that Glenn wanted. He wanted Christians to live in *unity* of the faith. It hurt him so much when quarrels came in and he sought and endeavoured to keep us all of one mind.

He had the knowledge of the God of *love* and the God of *peace* in his heart.

If there was one thing that marked the occasion both of his burial and thanksgiving service it was the number of Christians, old and young, who gathered to express the *communion* of saints; gathered to *salute* the memory of this dear brother whom we have loved, by whom we have been served and with whom we have served.

I read the last words that Glenn ever spoke on *Truth for Today* on Premier Radio. If you agree with him, say "Amen":

What a God we Christians have!

Amen!

Further Reading and Listening

READING

Full details of other books, magazines and calendars published by Scripture Truth Publications are available at our web site:

www.scripture-truth.org.uk

LISTENING

All programmes which have been broadcast on the *Truth for Today* radio programme at Premier Radio are available for reading, printing or listening to again at:

www.truthfortoday.org.uk

We encourage you to make use of this resource.

Lightning Source UK Ltd.
Milton Keynes UK

176591UK00001B/6/P